WALLOON WRITERS REVIEW

Ninth Edition

WALLOON WRITERS REVIEW

Ninth Edition

A collection of poetry, short stories, creative writing, and nature photography inspired by Northern Michigan and Michigan's Upper Peninsula.

Edited by Jennifer Huder and Glen Young

Walloon Writers Review Ninth Edition
©Walloon Writers Review, 2024
Petoskey, Michigan 49770
walloonwritersreview.com

Cover photography: ©Kate Allore *O'Neal Lake Speaking to Herself* 2024

Editors: Jennifer Huder and Glen Young

ISBN: 979-8-218-55465-1
ISSN: 2572-9683

CONTENTS

FOREWORD

Pushing off from the first night's camping spot, the three of us soon made our way into swells on Lake Huron.

Whitecaps broke over the bow of my kayak as I realized that paddling is often a paradox, as we move farther from one shore only to move closer to another, the last beach receding with each paddle stroke, while the beach ahead grows more near.

I'd never paddled this precise line before, so while I recognized the outline of the coast in front of us, I realized as well the joy of something new, remembering too how the night before we'd witnessed a comet just after sunset.

The poetry and the prose in this edition of Walloon Writers Review is all also all about the new, the wonders, seen and unseen, that focus for us the beauty and the mystery of Northern Michigan. There are observations here, as well as experiences, that illustrate how even in the familiar we can find the extraordinary, whether it is along the edge of a pothole lake or from the vantage point deep inside a boreal forest.

The writers here show us what it is to observe, whether hiking a deer trail or jumping off a swim raft. Each piece in the pages ahead peels back the visible, revealing an appreciation, sometimes collective, sometimes personal, for this precious landscape and the sometimes overlooked treasure.

Later, making our way along familiar rivers, my companions and I were hidden from drivers racing by on nearby roadways, though we could nearly reach out and touch the asphalt. Still, guided by eagles and serenaded by loons, we served witness to something that can only be seen if we slow down, if we pause, if we aim ourselves with the purpose of observation rather than acceleration. If we are open to not only what can be seen, but what is nearby but all too often unseen.

Enjoy the words and the images in the pages that follow, as our contributors highlight how the magic of Northern Michigan is all around us, if only we slow our pace.

– Glen Young, Co-Editor

© Elizabeth Fergus-Jean *Beneath the Surface* Mixed Media 2024

Biker

Ellen Lord

A week of summer love can feel like forever, riding backroads on a silver glide. So filled with rumblings…dangling dreams in silky air. But it's such a burden to love someone, to be loved. How you forget to slide into the silence of a solitary sky. You long to ride north on empty highways—as that iron-hued silk of the Ontonagon River calls you home.

fly fishing at dawn

catch and release

another memory

Does the Candle Know It's Sacred?
(A Poem About My Beeswax Candle and a Dragonfly)

Kate Allore

I
Building blocks for the light bearer, stolen from the castle
walls. If done mindlessly, the queen becomes currency. It is
rolled and molded and set aside, this light bearer, coming
to life only as its destruction draws near. Faint whispers
of buttercup and honey settle halfway between here and
there. Shadows of the setting sun move through the room.
Flickering light fills the void. Matter transforming.

II
I can perch comfortably on a mantle
of wood   or marble   or gold,
witnessing life and death
and all that in between;
the nursing baby, the changing seasons, the
composer composing, the lovers embracing,
                              a trip to the outhouse.

It's all the same to me.

III
It should be lighter out this morning.

It is April after all,
and the Robins have returned.
Damp soil smells creep in through

the tiny gaps under the door
while a blossoming forsythia keeps watch on the hill.
My hands wrap around
a steaming mug; I am not alone.

Melancholy and Hope
join me on the couch;
it is still dark out.

Hope lights a candle
as Melancholy whispers...

"It should be lighter out this morning".

IV
Is a candle born sacred?

or is it the cost of the candle
that appeals to the Gods?

Dragonfly grasps a blade of dune grass,
between two hands folded in prayer,

      bracing
           bracing —

What makes a Being sacred anyway?

© Kate Allore *Dragonfly* 2024

I Fell in Love with A River

Betsy Hayhow Hemming

Epiphany.

"A usually sudden manifestation or perception of the essential nature or meaning of something…an intuitive grasp of reality through something (such as an event) usually simple and striking."

Thank you, Merriam-Webster.

In other words, a great, big, sudden realization of something really important. At least that is what it means to me—for I fell deeply in love with a river, one that I hadn't really cared for much when I first was introduced. It took some time to come to that realization but when it emerged, like trout after flies, it was a doozy.

The river is called the Au Sable, meaning "of sand," and it flows majestically across northern Michigan. It has a storied history as an essential transportation link for Native Americans -- then logs -- before being recognized as one of the most pristine trout streams in North America. But I had the audacity to genuinely dislike this river when I met her, as she lured my fly fisher husband into her watery web. She also lured our daughters – even our dog – into her lair. I was the only holdout. Truth be told, I resented this river, this grip the river had on my loved ones.

Despite my doubts and fears, we bought a bit of land along the river, with a truly awful shack, broken and rotten and open to the skies – and critters. "Why would we want to buy this?" I asked in shock.

My husband beamed with excitement. "Because it's paradise," he responded. I didn't see that possibility for some time. I was quite convinced he was suffering from a significant mid-life crisis.

He coordinated the providing of essentials: a well, electricity, the all-important septic field. Awful shack transitioned to improved shack. We had a little compound along the river, with the one-room cabin, our pop-up trailer and a shed that became the finest outdoor bathroom in the county.

Giddy fisher husband bought CDs of cheesy fishing songs and urged his girls to sing along. He spent many a dark evening standing in his waters, rod in hand, speaking softly to the trout – and to the river. We girls snuggled in the little cabin, which certainly was more endearing than when I first set eyes on it.

Twenty years passed. The little cabin made way for a year-round river house. Slowly, oh so slowly, I warmed up to this body of water, who clearly had a very close relationship with Mother Nature. The sun bowed to the river most evenings in the most glorious of ways. I marveled at nature's offerings – the flap of the wings of the eagle heading downstream, rainbows casting their glow on the river, goose family wars and heron -- still and staring -- at river's edge. I found myself spending more time simply sitting on the riverbank, quite content to watch all the action.

Then one day in late summer, while floating in a fine Au Sable riverboat on a very chilly afternoon, I had the epiphany: that sudden perception of the essential meaning of something and in this case, it was my falling in love with a river, our place on the river, our life – everything. We're talking epiphany in every sense of the word. I wept tears of joy.

Her qualities became so clear. The Au Sable is a feisty wonder, with personality ups and downs that match the temperament of a teenager. This serene-looking body of water has a temper and isn't afraid to speak out when necessary – a quality I admire.

Peaceful and serene at one point and outrageous at another. It's dumped me in the river with nary a thought, then gently helped me through great grief. I realized how our entire family had found happiness, peace and wonder on this northern Michigan gem.

And on the day of the Epiphany, I told the river just how I felt: how grateful I was for all of her gentle and not-so-gentle teachings. How thrilled I was with her fine relationship with Mother Nature. That I belonged here. Life changed for the better on that chilly, windy day.

My darling husband had the word "Epiphany" carved in wood where it stands in the windowsill looking out on the river. Don't tell him, but I love the river as much or more than he does. The Au Sable grins her river grin, and carries on, offering massive life lessons to anyone willing to really get to know her. I am home.

© Betsy Hayhow Hemming *Sunset On The Au Sable River* 2024

Water Speaks

Kirk Small

Water Speaks woke to strange noises, a restless yammering just outside her front door. She could hear the rap-tap of goat hooves on the wooden porch. The chickens, too, were close. She listened carefully to the hens' low-pitched repetitive clucking along with the chicks' high-pitched peeps and tweets. Water Speaks understood the language, but she still was confused. The hens were not warning of a predator, but they were agitated, and the sound they made urged the chicks to stay close.

Curiosity got the best of Water Speaks. She threw off her blankets and started to slowly flex her arms and legs, willing the stiffness and aches away. She rose to her feet, poked at the fire and swung a metal pot filled with spring water above the embers. She reached into a nearby jar and grabbed dried leaves from the black cohosh plant. She rubbed the leaves together between her strong, callused hands and dropped them into the water. Water Speaks raised her palms to her nose and breathed in deeply.

"Ok. Let's see what the racket is about." When she opened the door, the goats and chickens crowded forward. "Gibichiwebin! Stop! What is wrong with you all?"

She pushed past the animals and surveyed the open space. Instead of her normal view, she saw standing water pooling and creeping forward. Water Speaks' eyes narrowed and she began to make a noise that sounded similar to the hen's agitated clucking. She stood on the front porch, naked except for wool socks, contemplating the situation. She shooed the animals away from her door, returned to the fire, and poured herself a hot cup of herbal tea. She took a sip and sighed with satisfaction. The goats and chickens continued to complain.

"All right, all right, I will be with you in a moment,"

Water Speaks took one last sip of her tea. She was going to have to get her socks wet today, and she hated wet socks. She finished dressing and then pushed her way through the animals. She frowned and mumbled a complaint to no one in particular as she took her first step onto the wet grass. She trudged through the rising water and headed toward the stream that ran from the high ground down to the marsh. The November morning was crisp, the water she waded through was cold, and her mood was frosty.

As Water Speaks approached the stream, she heard water babbling and she immediately knew the truth of the matter. She stood in ankle-deep water with her hands on her hips and looked the culprit in the eye.

"Boozhoo, Amik."

The beaver ignored her and kept putting the final touches on the earthwork dam that impeded the water from its natural course. Water Speaks appreciated beavers. She knew and was fond of most of the mating pairs that inhabited the nearby streams and marshes. She studied this beaver as it worked.

She watched for over an hour and finally said, "Well, this will not do."

Water Speaks mulled over the situation. This was a young male beaver, a bachelor. He was alone, but he was diligently working to make a safe, inviting place for a young female to join him, and if he found a mate, there would be no getting rid of them. If a mating pair established itself along this stretch of the stream, built a lodge, and had kits, they would defend their family and home to the death.

Many years ago, when her husband was still alive, a young male beaver attempted to dam the same area of the stream. At the time, she thought the whole thing was a bit amusing. She watched as Ahanu and the beaver matched wits. Both males were hard workers, and one would not be outdone by the other. Her husband would break up the dam by day, and the beaver would diligently rebuild it during the night.

Water Speaks shook her head as she remembered, "Men." She surely was not going to get in a pitched battle with this headstrong lovesick rodent.

She began to trudge back home and again said, "No, this will not do. He will have to go."

Water Speaks knew from personal experience that when a young male's desires are aroused, it can be hard to deter him from his chosen path. "I will just have to dissuade him somehow."

Water Speaks was a living almanac of the north woods, but the answer to this impasse befuddled her. She spent the day pondering the situation, but as sunset approached, she still did not have a plan to best the determined fifty-pound, three-foot-long rodent. Her socks, still damp, hung by the fire; they did not mock her exactly, but she pursed her lips and grumbled each time she looked at them.

She had just begun to doze when the coyotes started to caterwaul. A single yip, joined by others, became a rolling primal opus. Water Speaks knew this band of coyotes lived by the marsh, and she had seen the mating pair's pups grow to young adulthood over the summer and into the fall. The commotion caught the attention of a distant coyote band, and they too began to celebrate the coming darkness. These two canine groups were not enemies in any traditional sense, but the territorial boundaries that separated each band were a source of constant vigilance.

Water Speaks listened to the wild sounds echo to and fro. The last wild wail worked on Water Speaks' subconscious. First, just an inkling, and then a notion, that ripened into a plan.

"Well, if it's a pissing match Amik wants; then a pissing match it will be."

Water Speaks woke the next morning on a mission. She dressed and then rummaged through her carpet bag, finally pulling out a swatch of fabric about a foot and a half square. She left her home and hiked towards the marsh. When she reached her destination, she sniffed the wind. She moved windward, and every few steps, she took a deep, exaggerated inhale. She approached a lichen-covered granite boulder, kneeled, and snuffled first on one side of the boulder and then the other. She reached into her skirt pocket and retrieved the cloth. She rubbed the fabric first on one side of the granite and the other, then took one stride upwind and staked the material to the ground. Water Speaks stood, gave the staked fabric one last look, nodded with satisfaction, and returned home.

About an hour before sunset, Water Speaks returned to the boulder and the piece of cloth that she had staked down earlier. With one sniff, she knew her plan had worked. The two coyote bands had clearly defined territories. These territories were separated by an unseen boundary of scent markings that each group respected. Water Speaks had found the boundary and created an area of contention by shifting the border just enough to get both band's attention. The result was a new demarcation line and a completely coyote urine-soaked piece of fabric. Water Speaks removed the stake and raised the dripping cloth to her nose. She smiled with satisfaction.

"We will see how Amik likes sharing his home with the locals."

Water Speaks backtracked through the woods, past her cabin, to the beaver's dam. She snickered as she squeezed the urine-soaked cloth along the shore and on the earthen dam that abutted the embankment.

"What self-respecting male would try to raise a family so near such clear signs of danger?"

Water Speaks waited and watched, but two days later, it was clear that the score was still Amik one, Water Speaks zero. She stood with wet socks and watched him continue to toil; she bit back an oath when she realized that the beaver had begun working on a lodge.

Water Speaks waded back home and again repeated, "This just will not do."

The water continued to encroach on her small compound. She was worried about her bees. They were neatly tucked in the hives, but the rising water and the resulting damp would certainly threaten them. She uncovered one hive; the bees within were sluggish but still active. She spoke quietly to them, wishing them well, and assured them that she would protect them.

A single worker bee flew up and landed on Water Speaks' arm. She was stunned when she felt the barb enter her skin. She could not remember the last time she had been stung. This day was going from bad to worse. First, to be bested by Amik and then to be stung by what she considered to be one of the Great Spirit's most ingenious creations was humbling. She plucked the barb from her arm. She looked up into the sky and then back down into the hive.

"Mother, what am I missing?"

The pain in her arm began to ebb. She went back inside and decided to cheer herself up with a cup of tea. Today, to temper her mood, she would treat herself and add a spoonful of honey. She took a sip, savored it, and with a start, she started to laugh. She laughed so hard that she began gasping for breath and her eyes began to water. Water Speaks' mistake became clear to her in an instant; the Great Spirit had sent her a message in the form of a single bee sting.

The next day, Water Speaks left the cabin and went to see the progress that Amik had made since the day before. His pond was wider and deeper; the lodge on the far bank was beginning to take shape. She regretted the time that she had wasted. The Great Spirit had given her a sign and reminded her that humans spend too much time fighting nature's delicate balance.

Water Speaks took one last look at her furry adversary and then began to journey downstream. As she walked, she studied the vegetation along the stream's sandy bank. She paused to evaluate each tree as she passed. She circled an enormous red cedar and caressed the bark as if reading the tree's autobiography. She continued onward, and when she had been walking for about an hour, she saw a sign that gave her hope, a branch, bare of bark, bobbing along the water's edge. Water Speaks explored the riverbank and found birch and poplar saplings that had cut through at their base. The notched tips sticking out of the soil were a sure sign that Amik was nearby, but was it the right beaver?

Water Speaks hiked up her skirt and tucked its hem into her belt. She lowered herself on her hands and knees and started crawling along the shoreline. On all fours, she moved along the bank, loudly sniffing as she went. She had not gone far when she stopped and zeroed in on a particular section of the embankment.

She smiled and said, "Well, hello. I believe I have found you."

Water Speaks began to touch each plant and sapling until she found a waxy substance at the base of a birch clump. She scraped it onto a large, dried leaf and brought it to her nose. It smelled like vanilla. She knew that young female beavers excrete this oily perfume to entice prospective suiters.

Water Speaks got to her feet, re-adjusted her clothing, and began to walk back along the river to her home. Every ten minutes or so, she dabbed a bit of the waxy substance at the base of a tree. She did this until she was within sight of the dam that was the cause of her troubles. She knew in her heart that this fragrant trail would be irresistible to the fury bachelor and that he would move downstream to his destiny.

With one bee sting, the Great Spirit reminded her that nature can be tended and can be guided but not owned or controlled. At the end of this very long day, Water Speaks sat sipping hot tea and reveled in her fresh pair of warm, dry socks. She spoke out loud to no one in particular, "You can catch more flies with honey than you can with piss."

© Nancy Carey *Where the River Becomes the Estuary* 2024

Swallowtail Tiger's Trail

K. Matthew Springfield

Midwest meadow 'neath an azure sea
Antique fence trippin' second-growth trees
Taking in the tour, not rushing too fast
Gotta find our own heaven if this earth won't last

Days drag on in endless years
Spring poisoned winter, left a burning fear
Cold clawed back, so the black squirrels reign
Polar winds pushin' down south again

See a new bird singin' in the highest tree
Hey little bird you sound so free
Song dogs howling to a twilight moon
I'd join in too, but I sing off tune

Hear the mourning doves all say goodnight
Beat a bat outta hell if you step in sight
Lightning in the distance, won't pass close by
Firefly memories of a living sky

Woodchuck whistles in the forest choir
Hole in the ground by a tractor tire
Warm breeze blowin', what could it bring?
Swallowtail tiger, first one I've seen

Blackbird perched with wings dipped red
Calling so loud, tryin' to wake the dead
What the turtle says I won't recall
Talkin' up a storm, saying nothing at all

Bowfin on guard up a quiet stream
Catfish whiskers in a cut-bait dream
Raccoon gossip from the night before
Dumpster rich and nest egg poor

Wildflowers spread from where they're sown
Gardens turn green when no one's home
Dryad's saddle catching tawny light
Waitin' on a text everything's alright

Count every deer and turkey seen
Ain't November so they don't mind me
Leaning on a rusty metal spout
Neighbor's back forty, just hidin' out

Say songbird you sound so free
Swallowtail tiger hurry back to me
Sunset stars don't make a sound
Swallowtail tiger, comin' back around

Eyes closed tight, then count to three
Swallowtail tiger last thing I see
Midwest meadow 'neath a rising moon
Swallowtail tiger, headwaters of June

Wood Nymph

David James "DJ" Savarese

Her eyes and mouth are leaves.
If she could talk, she'd melt, I think,
or at least evaporate.
When the tree dies,
so does the Hamadryad--
in this case, Aigeiros,
denizen of the black poplar.
To say that she is bonded to her tree
is to believe too much in the spirit
of distinction: she *is* the tree,
that triangular, tooth-leafed cottonwood.
When Erysichthon cut down
Demeter's grove,
Limos bore like a beetle into his stomach,
becoming the need to eat.
And eat Erysichthon did
until he ate himself.
No chainsaw is ever happy.
Like the wood nymph, I live inside
the grain of speech, the would
of warning:
he who harms my sister
shall die of insatiable hunger.

The Three Runaways

Bridget Klaasen

If July is youth, August is truth and the truth is we are not young anymore. With this sad fact and the shortening hours of daylight, every September, we run away. We run away to different islands. My friend goes to one or another Manitou Island. She goes with her husband, they go back and forth, South Manitou one year and North Manitou the next. They are good negotiators. They have learned how to sleep in a tent. They go on hikes.

After two days she is ready to come home.

After five days, I am not. I go to Beaver Island. Alone. I stay in an Airbnb above a boat shop. I ride my bike. Alone.

We meet at the food co-op. She is a member. I am not. I ask her, "How can you imagine living on an island if you are staying in a tent?" She said she would never want to do that, to imagine living on an island. I am quiet because I can't imagine why else you would go to an island. We like to talk about people, not places. We talk about narcissists. We like to talk about them because once you get the hang of it, they are easy to spot. Personality disorders are easy, also. It is like identifying birds at a bird feeder. My husband has a bird feeder. He is a narcissist. He thinks he is a red cardinal. I think he is like a grey squirrel who hangs upside down and eats all the seeds. Grey squirrels are greasy. I have watched the bellies of grey squirrels swell.

"Don't you think it is odd that all your friends are married to narcissists?" I ask and she said,

"I never noticed that."

I don't believe her. I don't think there is anything she hasn't noticed. I have another friend (a sort of friend) who is on year six of learning a Debussy prelude. Her piano has its own room and a staff who checks its vital signs and the humidity in the room. It has disassemblers and transporters and reassemblers to move it at the request of a performer to a venue where no other instrument will do. If the piano were a horse, it would live in Dubai and fly in its own private jet. Alone. The (sort of friend) who's piano could win the triple crown said the friend across from me at the co-op is a true genius.

I think she means pure genius because there are few traces of carbon in her perfect brain.

My brain is like a pudding stone. Not common but not exactly rare.

I have another friend who wants to go to Beaver Island with me but she cannot. I have to go alone. I go alone because I like to write. I don't want anyone to know I like to write because I am afraid that if they knew, they could take it away from me. It has always been this way. It is like the joint on my left thumb. It is deformed and does not bend. You wouldn't know unless I show it to you. My mother was told I would never be able to play the piano with a thumb like that. It was meant to be a joke. She was greatly relieved. My family could not afford lessons, much less a piano to practice on. We could barely afford to place bets at the racetrack. Turns out, my crooked thumb was a stroke of good luck. It is perfect for the space bar.

The friend who wants to go to Beaver Island with me can't understand what I do for a whole week, alone, on an island. "What if it rains," she wants to know, "what do you do if it rains?" I told her I have a poncho I fished out of the Carp River (it must have fallen from a park service boat) and I wear it to the library. It is a long walk but the poncho keeps me dry. It is a beautiful library. It is built around a giant tree. The music room is wood paneled, with stained glass lamps and individually hand-glazed tiles. It sits next to a garden and children cut across a path from the school to use the computers. I told her I spent an entire rainy day there reading a volume of Jim Harrison's poetry.

"Jim Harrison, wasn't he a narcissist," she asked.

Oh, no, not you, too, I thought. "Just drunk, I think," I said.

Her children have moved away to be successful. One works for the federal courts in Philadelphia. Her office is on the fifth floor and has a view of the Liberty Bell. Her other daughter takes vacations in Indonesia. My friend has just settled her mother's estate. She is thinking about buying a new rock tumbler; her old one, she stored in the basement and it corroded in the dampness. She plans to make rock hunting her new avocation and has made a list of beaches: Van's Beach in Leland, a solid number one; somewhere in the middle, agates in Grand Maris; Beaver Island is closer to the top. Beaver Island is not known for its rocks, I tell her. In all the years I've been going, I have never found one worthy of the ferry ride home. I've found bits of pottery and broken tile—Salamanders, I tell her, Salamanders! I have found the most beautiful, rare salamanders on Beaver Island and I reach for my phone to show her and she stops me. "I don't want to hear about lizards," she said. She finds me frustrating. My daughter said I shouldn't take things so personally. She said it is not unusual to be misunderstood.

"Everyone should have their own island," I say to my friend who wants to go to Beaver Island with me, "Why don't you try Drummond Island? It is close, not a long drive, almost no ferry ride, and it is famous for pudding stones (although the way I bother her, I don't think she will like pudding stones)," and she asks if I would like to go with her and I say,

"No, I don't want to go to Drummond Island. There are too many gift shops. I can't imagine living somewhere with that many gift shops," and she is frustrated with me again because she didn't say anything about living on Drummond Island.

As though imagining and living are two different things. They are not. They are the same.

My friends and I ride the ferries to different islands. We go for different reasons. We return home for the same. We till our gardens, harvest our seeds, and cover the soil with mulch. In the last remaining days of September, we carry apple peels to compost piles and in separate kitchens, pour hot applesauce into jars, tighten the lids and bands, and set them on stacks of worn kitchen towels to cool.

© Michael Sipkoski *Tree of Life* Northern White Cedar, Roots 2024

The Road and the River

Hank Kaufmann

(Question: What's the difference between
a poor pipefitter and a rich pipefitter?
Answer: One paycheck.)

Friday, 24 June 1994:
Monied up, coming back from
four twelves in Rhinelander;
(it was the first I'd worked
in five months), the cooler
in the back of the pickup
filled with all the cans
of good, Wisconsin beer it
could hold. Stopping in
Eagle River, I picked up a
cover for the bar of my
chainsaw, but otherwise
just kept on WI 55, a two-lane
blacktop that plowed straight
north, then swerved right to
hug a gentle river,
named after a man
so savage he was knifed,
then eaten by other savages.

For miles there was just river
on the left and bush on the
right; then the river zigged
and the road zagged, and
Presto!
I was back in Michigan.

The road's forever.
Easy money always fades.
Rivers never end.

Lake Huron

Raegan Badik

<u>Fall Lake</u>
Multi-colored leaves
dance 'cross a lake clear as glass
under azure sky

© Raegan Badik *Lake Huron Through the Seasons* Block print 2024

An Acquired Taste

Gary Schils

"Beauty will save the world"
Dostoevsky from *The Idiot*

It is an acquired taste
to find beauty in simple things,
as learning to live within paradoxes
and not fear the mysteries hidden in complexity.

It is an acquired taste to love this world
even though it drifts towards disaster.
In the vast indifference of unknowns,
I am lifted by this acquired taste.

I am lifted from the jagged hole
of ugliness and despair,
as my lack of understanding seeks
curiosity rather than apathy.

As foul water filters and flows
through the Earth to find purity,
so too the beauty of simple things
flow through my troubled mind:

the aroma of phlox in the night air;
the slow saturation of stars in a darkening sky;
the strange shadows and shapes
of trees under a winter wolf moon;

a gentle breeze building into a blustery gale;
a rain-soaked Petoskey stone;
a yellow-shafted flicker feather;
a hawk spiraling towards the sun:

I rest my burdens upon
the beauty of these simple things
to remind myself exactly
where I belong.

The Old Hunter

Curt Benson

An old deer hunter sat in wet leaves and snow with his back against a tree. In one hand, he held Hemingway's *The Nick Adams Stories.* In the other hand, he held an apple. His rifle lay across his lap. He was motionless. He had just heard leaves rustle off to his right. He held tight, barely breathing. After five minutes or so, he relaxed. A squirrel, probably. The smallest things in the forest make the biggest noise. He smiled at the thought. He bit his apple with a loud snap in the quiet woods. He held up his book and began reading *Big Two Hearted River.* He was sitting in Michigan's upper peninsula, not far from the Fox river, where young Ernest Hemingway camped, fished, and hunted about a 100 years ago, and where many of the Nick Adam stories were set.

The old hunter wore a stained, knee length, olive green army raincoat with missing buttons and frayed cuffs. Over the raincoat, he wore a short blaze orange "camo" patterned vest. On his head was a weathered brown fedora. Beside him on the ground was a military style canteen that hung from his belt. Everything the old hunter wore, and the rifle he carried, was old and worn, except his boots. The raincoat his mom bought at a garage sale for $2 when he was in high school. The hat belonged to his dad who died in 1979. Underneath the raincoat, over his wool shirt, he wore a red nylon, goose down vest his wife made in 1973 from a Frostline kit. The canteen he bought 40 years ago at a gun show. His rifle, a .308 Remington Woodmaster, was a used gun he bought in 1981 from a guy who had placed a classified ad in the paper.

Only his boots were new and expensive, a birthday gift from his 43-year-old optometrist son who should not have spent so much. They were some sort of composite leather, very lightweight, yet insulated and warm. The old hunter marveled at them. All his life, whenever he had gone afield, he had worn cumbersome, thick brown leather boots with heavy rubber lug soles. His old-style boots were, so far as the old man understood, classic hunting boots. What else would keep your feet safe and comfortable while hiking through the northern Michigan forests and swamps? But these new boots. Well, they were nice.

The boots were delivered to his home just two months earlier by Amazon. They came with a card that said, "Happy Birthday, Dad – The World's First Boomer!" It was a tired joke, but something of a tradition. So long as he could remember, the old hunter called himself the world's first baby boomer. "Japan surrendered on August 15, 1945," the old hunter would say. "I was born just after midnight on August 16, 1945. That makes me the world's first baby boomer!"

He was a little cold, of course. It was November in northern Michigan which is just freezing wetness everywhere. As he read his book, the wind blew into his upturned raincoat collar and down his old Woolworth red and black plaid woolen shirt. He shuttered with chilliness and pulled a collar strap on his coat across his neck and buttoned it to the other side. He knew from 60 years of hunting that once the shivering starts, he'd have to stand up to walk off the chill. And that forces a reset. If a deer is nearby, stand up, and it won't be nearby any longer. You start hunting from scratch whenever you stand up. Whatever time you've spent sitting in a good spot is wasted. You start all over again.

He knew he was getting up. Twenty years ago, even ten years ago, the old man would have stayed put. But when he crept into his early 70's, the logic of sitting still in wet leaves and snow after the shakes began became increasingly elusive.

Getting up required a little planning. First, he leaned his rifle against the tree. Next, he leaned over to his right until his shoulder lay on the ground. He straightened his stiff, sore knees. He rolled over on his stomach. He put his gloved hands on the ground like he was preparing for pushups. He pushed upward while bringing his right knee under his waist. The idea was to put as little pressure on his left hip as possible. As he struggled upward, the pain in his hip hit and he exhaled sharply and let out a soft moan. As he continued upward, his hip hurt more, and his moans grew louder. Finally, halfway up, he grabbed the tree around with both arms and pulled himself upright as quickly as he could. Once standing, the old man stood still for a moment still clutching the tree and breathing heavily. When he finally straightened his back, it cracked. When he took a small step forward, his knee ached, and then the other. The pain in his hip briefly masked the other half dozen sharp aches in his body. Finally, the old hunter took a few more steps and shook his shoulders like a wet dog to beat back the cold.

The old hunter grabbed his rifle and slung it over his shoulder. He turned his torso this way and that, and finally decided to walk down the hill to the cedar swamp. When the hunting pressure was on, the deer headed for the swamp. And though he was alone in the woods, and there was no real pressure, after 60 years afield, the old hunter, like the deer he pursued, followed his own habits, his own patterns.

The swamp was a mostly colorless twist of grey and black, except for the thick green moss that grew everywhere. The old hunter paused, for just a moment, at the edge of this deep, sopping forest to enjoy the fresh pungent smell of cedar. He entered the swamp stiffly, slowly stepping over felled trees while twisting his ankles on trunks and branches protruding from the mud. He put his hands on upright trees as he labored over the downed ones.

He held onto slippery logs as he bent at the waist to push himself through low-slung branches. He pulled his legs up from sucking mud. His rifle was heavy. His breathing was heavy. The cold air hurt his lungs. His legs were so fatigued. He began to shiver again. His hip hurt. He slowed way down. He couldn't go on.

He stopped walking and leaned against a cedar tree, his eyes downcast, looking at those mud-covered new boots. He tried to control his breathing. He tried to get the pain out of his mind. When he looked back at his footprints, his only way out of the swamp, terror jumped in his chest. He turned his head this way and that way. For a second, for only a second, he did not know the swamp. His eyes widened; breathing grew heavy again. He clutched the tree he was leaning against and repositioned the rifle that was slung on his shoulder. Closing his red, wet eyes, he whispered,

"St. Michael," he prayed to the Archangel, a being he had not thought of in decades. "Please save me."

He worked to control his breathing. He worked to quiet his fear. In a few moments, he looked back again at his footprints, calmer now, but forlorn.

He turned his eyes upwards to the darkening sky.

"My last hunt?"

He saw himself at the O'Sullivan Funeral Home four months ago. He had been alone then too, briefly. He had asked his friends and relatives to clear the room for just a few minutes. Through his tears, he looked down at the face of his dead wife.

Now in the swamp, he turned around, and struggled back to his car, alone.

Lavender on my table

Cassie Lindholm

Fresh lavender rests in a glass on my table
A gift from your friend – sprigs of kindness flourish in her yard.
Outside, gray skies, soft as your faded flannel
We drive to the trail, silence gentle as hands held in the car.

Listen to the birds' good-morning serenading
The trees misty with sleep and summer dew
Strolling together, learning each other, talking and laughing
A dull day made bright in the company of you.

And like forgotten forecasted rain, a memory falls into place:
I've walked this same trail years ago, but, alone.
Peering back through sweet saplings to pining, desolate days
When I was rootless, new in town, in a home not yet home.

How strange, how wonderful – these
woods I once thought forlorn
Lively and full in a new perspective and time
Like leaves in spring, I too have been reborn
I have lavender on my table and love in my life.

© Tom Barrat *Pictured Rocks National Lake Shore near Munising* 2024

Where the Culture Started

for Lynn Spitznagel

Candace Lee

Chill wakes the furnace
radiators knock and snap their fingers
late fall when sourdough starter stirs
from its perch, rear of fridge but
once on a kitchen counter, hooch festers

No matter where a culture starts
whether an ancient Egyptian pot
or a village friend's heart
microbes nearby will alter it
tease out parmesan, sweet ethanol

until phantosmia of Leelanau
flips well-thumbed cards: one recipe
lifts its eyebrow, Tinklepaw's sourdough
tips scrawled in a *viola-hand*
that also placates and kneads of course

Gusts of snow slam a shutter
hot air hisses from valves
but the starter once re-fed snuggles
under cheesecloth as *mother sponge*
seems to rest, though a bubbly living thing

Tincture from first gestures: wild yeasts
off hands of bakers wiped on aprons
lactic acid colludes with bacteria
leavening yeasts join flour water
soon loaf pans criss-cross cast iron slots

nurtured from the recesses of an era
these chambers of iron fins
show an appetite for hard work,
mounds of dough grow pregnant
topping rims, generations

A niece lifts one, then tiptoes
toward the oven, prays it bakes
like a rounding ripe souffle
breathes in fungi as family sips cider
tea, swigs beer, conviviality

When bread bakes
all nostrils flush and twitch
hot water pipes creak, gurgle
pulse warmth throughout
each Victorian floor

By now, manifolds below windows
become settees, upon each
a couple kids chew buttered chunks
hunched leavening over books
snow piling up behind shoulders
nearly Victorian characters themselves

Wallowing in Mushrooms

Candace Lee

Wanderlust in woods near Shalda Creek
among interdunal swales
eager for morels, black trumpets, shaggy mane
craving a nutty scent
just one yellow-foot chanterelle
a tinge of lavender on blewits

Ivy on the contrary flaunts, flings itself upward
hooked nails of a vixen glisten
winking with more than dew
pole dancing from stems
scarlet as a harlot on shelf concha

distracts from stumpies
cuddles of honey fungus
ensnared creatures
busier absorbing and decomposing
than brandishing its polysaccharides

but our hunter seeks antioxidants
admires monstrous mycelium

We find her prone on a cot
dipping mushroom quiche in Armillaria gulyas
while blisters weep on satin sheets
just for giving into an itch
dreaded curse, base of dead oak

yet again she stands to cook her find
with shallots and garlic in white wine.

© Karen Reasoner *Finding Fungi at Higgins Lake* 2024

Muskellunge as Muse

Gary Schils

Full June moon—star pricks of light come
and go like fireflies in the fabric of night.
Imbued by pale ale and camp smoke
a man trolls alone, his specter driven

by canoe and paddle j-stroking
the inky waters of Lost Lake.
A muskellunge lurks at weeds edge,
lacking cruelty yet keen to kill.

Seduced by a form weaving
through dim waters, the fish
smashes the lure, driving
hook into boney jaw.

Until the fish is spent
love and war tango on taut monofilament.
As rod and reel pump and moan
the fish is drawn to net and netted.

A dull stare emanates from primal eye,
patient for death if death should come.
A rocking by the tail brightens gills.
The beast's blood restored.

To bring time to fulfillment
the fisherman releases the fish
for death of one Muskellunge
is death to all the fishes in all the sea.

As the fish descends,
Li Po looks east for a sign of morning,
and, in a pulsating moment,
a loon's cry erupts over the entire earth.

Soft Trails: A Reverie of South Manitou

Max Old Bear

Soft, my footfalls in the spongy duff of the forest floor
one spring morning. Leeks crushed into pungency by a
wayward step. A canopy of maple leaves absorbs most
sounds like the veery's "wheet, wheet wheeeuw" though
not the easily recognized "cher tee, Cher Tee, CHER
TEE" of the "teacher bird". Nothing else like it in the
woods, this call of the ground nesting oven bird.

Blues of an indigo bunting dart above ferns, so intense
among subtle greens. The air, too, is soft on a hike this early
in a morning passing by trout lily, hepatica, bloodroot,
great patches of Jack-in-the pulpit. Swaths of trillium by
the thousands. I search for the variegated variety with such
a broad green stripe it camouflages their white petals.

Any hiker is humbled upon entry into a towering,
giant cedar forest. Trunks so large it would take
several people, arms outstretched, to encircle one.
But there are no others, only mossy fallen cedars
becoming a bed, nursery logs for a new generation.

Now any sign of trail is left behind, as the loose sand
of steep western dunes imposes on the forest. A gradual
smothering that I also feel while catching my breath.
Climbing the dune, I grasp branches of half buried trees.
Again and again, I must find foot purchase in the sand.

Upon reaching the high dune plateau, my spirit lifts with a
clearer view stretching out to the horizon. Among patches
of dune grass: orange dune lily, yellow hoary puccoon,
blue harebell nodding in the breeze, pale pinks of beach
pea. Close by the scent of sand cherry announces itself.

A triumph to find Pitcher's thistle in pastels of leaves, its flowers
a creamy hue, maturing and flowering only once in its five
to eight year life. Wee mice tracks lace among them, red-tail
hawks circling above. And some say sand dunes are barren!

And then, hiking to the western edge of the dunes
looking far down the bluff at Lake Michigan below.
In the distance, Washington Island in Wisconsin.
And still, a bright, full day yet to come.

© Becky Jensen *Michigan Summer* 2024

Lake Michigan Synecdoche

Brenna Dean

I used to hold so much fear
   for you. That indifference.
       The way you would not
          slam on the brakes
    if a deer stood frozen
  in your headlights.
You'd just barrel through,
   even hit the gas
       if you'd already planned to.
        There's always been a soul struggle
     with indifference. A desire for others
  to care about us,
the heartbreak of realizing
  some don't. Perhaps
     because they don't know us.
      Perhaps because
   they do.
  But as I sit on this dry stone
upon your shore, and you approach gently,
   fade away several feet from my own,
     there's comfort in your indifference,
      too. To face the water
    and not wonder if it finds me ugly.

To allow my face
to reflect every thought.
  To clamber off this rock,
      no embarrassment,
          no performance.
      Presence I only attain
  in the indifference
of you.

Wistful Return

Anne M. Rashid

You want to go back to the indigo bunting
chirping on the telephone wire
above Wildwood Road where cars go by
kicking up clouds of dust, only slowing
when they see you walking alone.
You want to wave to be neighborly,
but also encourage them to take
their time and not cover you in dust.

You want to go back to the two coyotes
trotting down Mitchell Road
in the middle of the night, not caring
about you stopping and watching.
You could have reached out
from your station wagon window
to pet one of them going by.

You want to go back to Lake Michigan
and the waves hitting the shore—
the rocky shore—where you found stones
to carry with you to help you remember
this slender moment of calm.

Back in this working world, your northern haunt
seems so far, almost imaginary.
It helps to remember it exists—for the next time
you can retreat from papers and grading
and meeting after meeting after meeting.

Ready Waters

Skip Renker

I've walked beside northern waters
all my life—Bear Lake, Walloon,
Higgins, the Little Manistee,
the Big Two-Hearted, and Lake Michigan,
where a distraught Odawa woman,
the story goes, cried out to the Great Spirit
after her partner died, threw herself
from a Hartwick pine onto a jumble
of rocks in the shallows.

My thoughts move in rhythm with my steps
and the sounds of moving water, ripples
of emotion, speculations, memories
that surface, then slide back under,
as of bleeding Martha in one of my rare
unhesitating moments—I dived in
and rescued her. I gave myself wholly
to water that day, and on another,

twenty years married, a new love
flooded me, a catastrophe of wonder
and terror that tumbled a home,
a marriage, and several lives
miles downstream. My tears often
hesitate, though my deeply wise
grandmother used to call them
the ready waters of the soul.

Today I walk Crooked Lake's south shore,
longing to experience a soul fed
by inexhaustible springs of forgiveness
and hope, but for the moment I'm glad
for the morning's still waters, reflecting
red-tinged clouds and a low-flying heron.

© Nancy Hayes *Red July 24* 2024

708 Miles

Storm Ainsley

Fall
isn't quite the same between
time zones. When is dusk?
When I left. Dark after mile of stoplights to highway.

It was 18:30 in Chicago, 19:30 where
        I cross line just after Gary, but for sure when I hit
Michigan border. It'll be about an hour.

Half moon side straight up&down
is three hours and off that second highway later
cocked to the side like a cradle. Why does it take
82 mph to feel I'm moving?

In Chicago, leaves away from buildings burn first,
the rest catch on.

0:22 Here
Winter's teeth sink deep
enough to draw blood
first taste: freezing rain

Gunshot crackle keeps us from the thickest trees.
Shadows rise from ditches, fields glow gold to brown, brush bristles.
I never find the corn maze
or the graveyard

my sense of season is tuned to the wrong place
trying to claim me for a dance
step I was supposed to forget.

22:47 heading back, 21:47 on my clocks
        Hit up my gas station for free coffee
28.75 in the tank. Last rounds snaked north through town
instead of out the South End, a difference of 162A to 153.

The road is heavily guarded
but I'm tired enough not to speed much
or sing along.

Where thoughts touch
my insides scatter leaves

708 miles doesn't feel like much
$93.67 does.

Return, Afternoon

(After Hughie Lee-Smith's *Après-Midi*)

CJ Giroux

I am called back to "our" beach, its pennants wind-whipped
like the tangled tails of stallions stampeding.
Despite still water, mothers warn of riptides—
thunderheads double and tumble, sidling
east, where blues, betrayed,
will become grey. The peninsula is a sleeping toddler,
her shoulders covered with Coppertone,
a moth-chewed picnic blanket.

I just can't be done with you.

I sneak beyond torn caution tape, marking the city park's limits.
Condo construction has been halted, again,
and where we last kissed, the dunes rise,
fall like a child of divorce
promised progress, change, haven, home (but whose?).
Drainage pipes resurrect civil war cannons,
waiting to be lifted, fed, filled; I imagine blocks, bricks,
beams rearranged; for now, they are a Lego building broken,
pain underfoot at midnight.

I just can't be done with you.

Wearing sweatpants you claimed the color of merlot,
I am in a no man's land; I'm an aluminum skiff
tethered to shifting shore, weathered wood.

As much as I shake out your old beach towel—
its center filling, curving like tissue paper on a kite
straining to separate from its balsa frame—
sand remains: a reminder, a broken treaty.

I just can't be done with you.

© Pamela Atsoff *August Glory* 2024

Angel Revery

Thomas Ford Conlan

Heard on high
the diminutive Chickadee answers my whistle

A breeze between tall trees in the forest
carries a tune to soften my thoughts

A presence unseen
calms restless waters

Sometimes a man must become an Angel
if only for a moment

Angels walk amongst us
But Angeling is a hard life, unseen, only felt

Angels cannot pretend
rewards hide in the bushes

I suspect that Chickadees
are Angels in bunches

A bright red Cardinal came on a September morning
and has returned each morning since

The male seems more Angelic
stares back and sings

The Female often picks seeds shaken to the ground
a warmer brown, she speaks of home

An old man carries a staff
a crooked, varnished maple branch

a Genesis stone, a prism, adorns the peak
sunlight changes colors against an azure sky

An old Friend walks up the lane
knocks on my door

Regarding Cardinals,
I believe

a feather light red bird
carries a message

from a place we cannot see
from a time we cannot know

Beliefs are unseen clues
unsubstantiated feelings

What is real?
The Cardinal at my window

My head buried down at my desk
in the work of my own musing

As I look up at the world
he is there out my window watching me

His red glorious
amidst lake effect snowflakes

A fundamental Crack as
a polished ash baseball bat meets a horsehide hardball

View reality through the
prism atop an old man's staff

An aged aspen leans out over a winter hayfield
a Bald Eagle alights upon a branch

Angel of death hovers over some small creature
he hunts from his perch

I would welcome an Eagle
to toll the bell

but would prefer a Red-tailed Hawk
or perhaps a bright red Cardinal
or a joyful bunch of Chickadees

when my time comes

"Let The Moss Take It All Back"

John Lennon

Let the moss take it all back
Down to the studs and
Lonely promises.
Tomorrow was built
On a loose canon:
>Stolen homes and
>Vacant bird's nests.
>Whose children are these?
>Crying, sitting under the burned tree
>They stretch arms down down down
>Back to black and aching earth
>Under a loathsome winter that wants
>Nothing
>More than to see it all begin again.
>Beg for it to smolder under
>The branches wrenched too soon
>So that life might breathe small again.

Cathedral for the Winged

April DeOliveira

On the front porch of my grandparents' tiny,
cozy house—
a mere speck on a map in vast Northern Michigan,
in sleepy, slow-rhythmed Chatham—
dangles a hummingbird feeder,
alluring, cherry-hued and flower-scrolled,
a cathedral for the winged, its thick sugary substance
the water of life.

Gray-Green Female zips to the cathedral,
hovers, wings slicing the barren air
outside one of four open entrances.
She perches.
Wings halt.
A lowered guard shrouds her
in vulnerability.
She inserts her beak, an eager and hopeful
offering in the dusky blue misted morning,
and drinks life in desperation.

Red-Throated Male's buzz in the distance
crescendos, bells clamoring in warning.
No time to react, Gray-Green Female
is body slammed away like she'd never belonged.

Levitating nearby,
displaced exile,
pure fury the wind beneath her wings,
she strategizes, jets to an entrance on the other side.

She perches. Drinks.
The Earth sighs with dewy breath,
but not for long.

Red-Throated Male abandons his stolen territory.
There's abundant room yet only room for him.
He swoops down upon Gray-Green Female.
She barely escapes by the feathers of her beak
to a neighboring tree,
sacred refuge of timbered shadow and leafy buckler.

Red-Throated Male, belly distended with another's portion,
retreats to an adjacent bush.
And waits.

Gray-Green Female carpe diems,
soars on pained thirst to a cathedral,
to a life,
that invites her in against this stumbling block.

Nothing less than misguided want propels
Red-Throated Male onward now.
The two collide.
Their thud emanates through the yard
and falls like an aching prayer
onto a wooden altar sheltered beneath stained glass.

© Michele Austin *Composite Flight Plan* 2024

Casting for Ghosts

Stephen Hooper

At least once every season I try casting for ghosts.

I've heard stories; rumors, of this place. Old-timers throw the name out in barside conversation, reminiscing about days past when the fishing was good in every spring-fed backwater. A four pound, twenty inch brook trout in a pond this size? Brookies that size are a rarity anywhere. A few lucky folks have had the fortune to catch one of their "coaster" cousins while trolling on Superior. Anyone who would have caught a wild fish that size in a stream or beaver pond around here is probably no longer alive to talk about it. Now, fish that size only are caught when the hatchery plants its retired broodstock; their fins and tails worn and frayed from years in a concrete raceway. My first "big" brook trout was one of these, caught in an old, flooded iron mine periodically stocked with fish, though I didn't realize it until years later. It would have been half an inch longer, too, if its tail was entirely intact.

But old Lewis Pond has been forgotten; discarded. Kids who fished here with their grandparents grew up, moved south, and traded in trout worms and rubber boots for diesel trucks and bass boats. The last of the old-timers who fished it have been gone for more than twenty years, and it's around that same time the DNR gave up on it and began devoting their efforts to other, more productive waters. Stocking trout in remote lakes is expensive, both in terms of money and labor. Few are the people who would voluntarily hike in to fish such a "marginal water", to quote the email reply from the local Fisheries Biologist. The water started to get too warm. Mining operations and a golf course lowered the local water table. The inlet is far too clogged with sediment to realistically support any spawning activity. The eggs would suffocate in the sand. The pond just doesn't have nearly enough groundwater feeding it to keep temperatures down and oxygen up. The trout, he wrote, have probably long died off without any descendants to replace them. Eaten by otters or herons. Probably overrun with stunted bullheads, creek chubs, and suckers by now. Maybe a few bluegill if I was lucky. "Frog water", another dismissive descriptor.

After hours scouring satellite imagery of this place on Google Earth over the past couple months I still wasn't sure what I'd find. The lack of information is, admittedly, part of what drew me in. As incredible a feat of human innovation the internet is, few places on the planet remain shrouded in mystery. But despite being within a fifteen minute drive from town, places like this still are a type of wilderness to most, if only because little to no information exists on the internet. It's too small to be listed in any of the spiral-bound map books found in local sporting goods departments. Not even an estimate of depth. Asking around isn't much use. Folks who fish for brook trout are reclusive and reluctant to share intel; often for good reason, as productive trout waters are becoming a rarity. No photos of the place either, aside from satellite imagery. I'd probably have better luck going door-to-door up Third Street and asking if the old family photo album had any shots of grandpa and his fishing pals at the pond.

I park the truck in an inconspicuous spot just off the main road. There's still about a half mile walk down a well-worn hiking path that passes along the ridge above the pond. Despite being dressed in chest waders and an overstuffed vest, I try to not draw attention to myself. There are still a couple hours until it gets truly dark, but I pack a headlamp anyway. I feel ridiculous having brought a fly rod in the truck; moreso as I unpackage a new tapered leader and tie on a little blue-winged olive. I pause and consider whether to carry a net, as it conveys unrealistic - laughable - hopes and expectations. But I sigh, remind myself no one else is around to see, clip the net to my vest, and set off down the trail.

Early summer evenings in this part of the country are simply stunning. The sun is still fairly high above the tree line even though it's getting close to nine. It's still nearly seventy degrees out. Humid too. The spring peepers are out in full force and I know they'll only get louder as I approach the pond and the sun goes down. The mosquitoes don't bother me much anymore. When I was a kid I couldn't stand them. My mom still plans her summer activities based on how "buggy" it is outside. I even find the smell of bug spray pleasant. For me, the unmistakable scent of summer is a blend of pine, mowed grass, fern, woodsmoke, and DEET. The neuropsychology of the senses is fascinating. No photo or video; no virtual reality experience could quite trigger the same memory response as this combination of sights, sounds, and scents. After getting caught up in thought for a while, I'm suddenly standing atop the ridge above the pond. The hemlock stands are too thick to glimpse the water from here. I find something resembling a deer trail, then ducking beneath boughs and breaking through dead branches, I follow it down and around to a marshy part of the shoreline.

From where I'm standing, ankle-deep in the sulfurous muck along the shore, the pond looks like dozens of others I've visited over the years. The whole thing can't be more than an acre or two. Such an arbitrary measurement - how far do I need to cast to actually land my fly in the water and not on a lily pad? Tag alders line most of this shore; tall pines and steep banks on the other side. Water lilies are blooming in the shallows, giving way to a relatively small area of open water in the middle. Water striders skid across the surface. Some tiny flying insects I don't recognize are flying in a complex formation just a couple feet above the water. There's a mallard and her babies near the shallow inlet at the far end of the pond, quietly diving into the mud to feed. The whole scene is familiar but a bit unsettling, like photos of abandoned amusement parks or malls. Or an open-casket funeral for a distant relative. I've brought my rod and a couple flies not because I planned to catch anything, but out of respect for the dead.

I stand and watch the pond for what feels like an hour, although it's probably only five minutes. The water is very clear, only appearing dark on satellite maps because of the muck below. I dip my hand in and it's colder than expected. And so, like a funny memory shared during a eulogy to lighten the spirit, I strip out some line and make a little roll cast out just beyond the edge of the lilies. The tiny fly floats for a while. I leave it out there as I make my way a little further down the shoreline, one hand grasping the tag alders in case the muck gets too deep. I find a break in the thick brush where I can make a short back cast. Another couple casts out, a bit further each time. I leave the fly still for a while, then try gently twitching it. Surely *something* would take this fly, even if it was a creek chub. Ironically, I once fished a stretch of the East Escanaba with dry flies and only caught chubs; then switched to a spinning rod and worms and caught brook trout. Not that I expected anything, but I have a hard time reeling in and calling it quits on the little dry fly.

It's getting darker. The sun has dipped below the trees now. I only brought a couple flies in my pocket, so I snip off the blue-winged olive and clumsily tie on a black wooly bugger that's probably big enough to hook one of the fall kings down on the Manistique. Silly, I tell myself. Here are some final words of comfort as the casket is lowered into the earth. I make a long cast out into what I'm assuming is the deepest part of the pond, letting the fly sink while I count twenty, before I start to strip in line in short bursts. I'm only half-paying attention and it takes me a minute to realize what's happening. All of a sudden and all at once, there's no room for confusion - my line is moving out into deeper water and a fish is pulling drag.

It doesn't feel like a brook trout, or really any sort of inland trout. I've been fortunate to catch enough brooks, browns, and rainbows to know what they feel like on the other end of a line. This feels more like the fat lakers I've reeled in fishing on my buddy's salmon boat. It's heavy and doesn't want to come up to the surface. Just a steady, dogged pull deeper and deeper. My excitement fades a little, though, as something doesn't feel quite right. There's no way this is a trout. I recall the time up in Seney when my buddy, standing on a fallen tree laying across the stream, thought he hooked into a real dandy only to pull in a big old white sucker. But why - and how - would a sucker take a wet fly unless it was right on the bottom?

This rod is my great-grandfather's, a little wooden number labeled "O-Fish-Al, Point Sporting Goods, 1955", only really suited for the little log jam brookies up on the Yellow Dog that rarely grow over nine or ten inches. It's bent over in a hoop like those iconic silhouettes of fly fisherman landing their catch that adorn the covers of outdoor magazines. The leader, tapered down to two pounds at the end of its nine feet, is too light for this fish. Is it snagged in the weeds? There is movement again. I let the fish pull out more drag but my reel is almost out of line. I reel in a bit and gently try to pump the rod to move the fish up. It moves up closer to the surface. It feels lighter now - the fish is swimming toward me. It approaches the surface and I see a quick flash of movement.

The times I've been deer hunting, sitting in a dark blind as the light struggles to breach the horizon, it's deceptively easy to mistake some maple twigs for antlers. If only I could *will* them to be so. At that moment, with the last of the evening light fading around the pond and the chorus of peepers almost deafening, I knew exactly what I was seeing. The fish turned upright and for a small fraction of a second revealed the unmistakable yellow spots and red speckles against a dark, almost black, body. Some sucker! Never trust a fisherman to give you an accurate estimate of length without photographic evidence; but this fish was well over a foot, probably near a foot-and-a-half. My heart rate speeds up again. I slowly reach around with my left hand to grab the net. The fish dives and starts to run again. Foolishly, I try to stop it in its tracks and turn it around. Suddenly, all goes weightless. The line goes slack. Shit.

I don't remember much of the hike back out of there. My heart is racing. I think about the times I've nearly collided with a deer out on a dark winter road. The adrenaline hit is delayed and only comes once the scare is over. There's really no one around to appreciate or believe what just happened. None of my fishing friends care much for trout, especially when it involves any kind of hiking, and when I can coerce them into coming along they prefer a worm and bobber. Heck, that's how my brother caught that fifteen-incher out of Midway Pond last spring while I got skunked with flies. For now, just a ghost story.

It's now quite dark and I'm second-guessing as I climb back into the truck. Memory is fickle; unreliable. The more a memory is replayed, the more muddled it becomes. Honest eye-witness testimony is known to be inaccurate over half the time. Did I really see the spots? Yes. *Definitely* yellow spots. Maybe it was a little pike that somehow migrated way upstream from Partridge Lake. Yes, that's probably what it was.

"That does make more sense," I say out loud, trying to explain away what I know I really saw.

I pull into the driveway, peel off my waders on the porch, and walk in the door, exhausted and smelling strongly of hemlock and bug dope. My wife is on the couch with a book. The kids are asleep. Out of obligation, she asks if I caught anything.

"Almost," I mumble, out of breath.

"Almost."

© Pamela Atsoff *Misty Morning Reflection* 2024

Pickerel Creek in Summer

Katherine Roth

It's just a creek on the map—
we drive narrow dirt roads for miles to find it
lower our kayaks and begin to paddle
but once upon the water,
we discover it's a river
winding through grasslands,
cattails and wild rice hug the shore

I want to belong to this world that has no need for words,
just this close embrace
as the wind bends
waist high grass
and it beckons like a hand
like a song—
like the black bird cry

A beaver lodge appears--
with sharp chewing and mud slapping they've claimed this river
teeth marks on each log
and the pond waits beyond—
it's what they needed
what I've been searching for
this depth of water, this protected stillness

I put my paddle down

Renaming the Pileated Woodpecker

Milton J. Bates

The cap for which it's named may be
its least distinctive feature, worn
by many red-headed species,
including members of our own.

Call it *Chisel-Billed* instead,
for the trenches and rectangles
it gouges into trees, for the chips
that litter its workshop floor.

Call it *Dexterous* for the claws
that ratchet the bird up a tree
or dangle it like a chickadee,
upside down, from suet feeder.

Call it *Pterosaurus* for its
head in profile, its piercing
Mesozoic call, its reptile
scales refined into feathers.

Call it *Medicus* for the way
it hunts down carpenter ants,
making the rounds of our pines
like a doctor with stethoscope.

It taps and listens, working up
and around each trunk. We are
relieved, when it flies off, to know
our trees have passed their physical.

© Don Spezia *Natural Beauty* 2024

a buzzard flies us in | as we leave, a doe

Sarah DiViasmeṇi

*

'black raspberries trail | fat pale blossoms'
this beating-heart place has a name

at the car I guess how to dress | I wrap a scarf
around my neck against the cold canopy shade

my path-finding friend | he threads the forest floor
brings us close along an upturned tree | roots showing

moss & dirt converse | crouched | I cup
cool water but not to drink
in the language of streams | we are understanding

we are wreathed by living things | love-calling birds sing
high in the hemlock boughs | he knows what is poisonous &

unshy with each other we chew evergreens | on the
creek bed we laugh | comfortable to rest

*

blue paint marks the beginner's threshold | this beginning
is not the same as being born | more like finding

a turkey's egg | also blue | abandoned to a nest of cedar rot
it has its own history | but life is more than that

here | I learn the names of edible mushrooms
coral | oyster | chicken of the woods | wild

strawberries at my feet bear fruit I have never seen
& in praise of solitude | in favor of solitude

I come back alone | pull ripeness to my hand
my old horizon clears | now the horizon before me

August

Christopher Gerst

First fire of the year
Leaves of red orange and gold hue
Cider pumpkin moon

Chant

Doug Pfaff

There's a hum in the earth
as it collects itself. All the clouds giving back
all the waters from the months behind.
Children laughing in the ages of leaves,

joyful in the softness of the season's death.
Place your ear to the ground,
the saturated earth, and feel the hum,
the low Gregorian Chant of it

as wetness seeps into rock, and light abandons its post.
Then, climbing like a thief, the wetness
robs the earth of itself and steals away
into your knees.

And the season lives on
a little longer having not yet
captured all it needs
to become winter

© Doug Pfaff *Milkweed* 2024

Shinrin-yoku

Kristin Bartley Lenz

When hope feels like a hollow log,
carved from rain and rot,
a cavernous tunnel
hiding horrors, I gather
star shaped leaves,
sticky pinecones,
furry husks cradling
beechnuts. I gather
capped acorns,
spiraling samaras,
milkweed fluff.
I gather my wits
and my whimsy.
I gather my breath
drawn deep from my belly.
And I stuff
that dark, damp cavity
like a Thanksgiving turkey.
I leave it to bake
in the murky forest,
through sleet and snowfall and critters
scampering, scavenging, burrowing.
And when again I visit, I'm buoyed
by the smattering of fungi springing

from the decay; tiny white ears
listening   to the questions
rising
from my footsteps.

*Shinrin-yoku is the Japanese practice of "forest
bathing" to promote physical and mental wellbeing.
My favorite place to "forest bathe" in northern Michigan
is in the woods near my house on Walloon Lake.*

© Elizabeth Fergus-Jean *Oak and Maple* Mixed Media 2024

Morning Tea

Ellen Lord

All winter long there is
an old chair by the window—
one aubergine pillow
rimmed in lace.

Two beeswax candles
aglow before dawn
bode the arrival
of another blue hour.

Our window looks out
on a pinewood forest
and sometimes up
to a clear sky

© Tamar Charney *Around the Bay* 2024

if I beg your hands into a bowl

Sarah DiViasmeņi

for tart black raspberries-
means I'll feed you while you're helpless,
I'll do it without knowing,
I'll whistle low songs about Coyote,
let loose the sound of my *real* laugh,
get down inside the cedars to scrounge
for bluejay feathers and little speckled shells,
and there, I'll catch my breath
at a vision of three perfect knots

I've never been this close to home
or fruition.

It's Not Sodapop

Mary Anna Scenga Kruch

A pencil or two
are stuck in the ground
clumps of grass

that missed their targets
lay abandoned
not one stayed to see

the afternoon light
dappling the trampled lawn
through the shade

of their maple
but that's what stays with her
she sighs

retrieves copies
of *The Outsiders* whose parts
they had quarreled over

gathers pencils
a lost barrette
understands it's not

Ponyboy or Sodapop
but Lake Michigan
that tugs them away.

Clarinet Island

Susan (Phare) Boback

Written in reflection of her Junior High years in Ishpeming 1965 – 1967

I still remember getting my B Flat Bundy Clarinet, new reeds, a lesson book and my very own fold-up music stand. The summer session of Beginning Band at C.L. Phelps School in Ishpeming was six weeks long for beginners entering the sixth grade. Each section met separately until about the last 2 weeks when we had learned the fundamentals enough to try to play as one group.

"Practice makes perfect," the saying goes. It happened every other day after school or on the weekends at my house. Practicing was something that was understood. You practiced. There was no question about it or no way to get around it. This was a time that being part of a musical family could be a disadvantage, at least from a kid's point of view. I could only imagine the many more fun things to be doing.

My best friend Kim and I spent many days squeaking and squawking as we both learned to control our lip pressure, our embouchure, on the mouthpiece. Besides having the ability to read music and use the right keys, having a good embouchure was a major reason why your music was on tone or was flat.

Kim's father was the caretaker at what was then known as the McCormick Tract, which was north of the Peshekee River, off of US 41 West, between Champion and Michigamme in Michigan's Upper Peninsula. This privately owned acreage had lodges, docks, and boating facilities, which very few people had access. Some of the fondest memories of my childhood are the times we spent learning to play our clarinets at the McCormick

Tract. Kim's father would tell us to take the rowboat out and go over to a little rock island to practice our clarinets. He told us that if we went over there, we would have privacy, and no one would bother us. What a thoughtful dad! I only recall rowing over there once, but not getting out because the ground was not level enough to set up a music stand and start playing. Her dad even called this little rock outcrop, "Clarinet Island," which we considered quite an honor.

This little rock island's new name was never made official, like a location on a plat map or anything like that. It was quite a while before we realized that it was not our privacy and lack of interruptions that her father was really interested in finding for us. But his goal was the need for peace and quiet, as much as his own sanity, from listening to our squeaking and squawking as we learned to play our B Flat Bundy Clarinets.

And now, these many years later, my own granddaughter is learning to play a clarinet. I wonder what "Clarinet Island"— a soundproof, choice spot for practicing —her parents find for her!

© Amy Pendell *Night Majesty* 2024

Grounded

Ralph James Savarese

In Northern Michigan, I have a neighbor
who purposefully sited his house so that

it didn't have a view. "Views," he said,
"were for gods or rich people. Same thing!"

(I was there helping him put in his ridge beam.)
He wanted to be surprised, he explained,

by the ordinary: a turkey vulture waddling
like his grandfather in the yard, the trees

in autumn turning the color of his son's hair.
Why be a lookout, I understood him

to be saying? Why spot the fronts as they
come in: cancer, divorce, bankruptcy—every

form of human weather? Discover the snow
as it hits your face. A view is a divining

rod for the ego, as horizontal as a lakebed
or corpse. "I'm happy being the pawn of fate,

moving my one little square. Let the queen
or bishop, like a bolt of lightning, take me out.

Live small!" he yelled—we were struggling
with the beam—"so that death is

nothing more than a raccoon in your garage."
So much for laconic Michiganders…

I live

above this guy, at the top of the hill, my house
a post-and-beam soliloquy. With its wall

of windows, it looks the way my wife looks
now with three pairs of glasses on her head!

Or maybe it resembles that telescope
in Hawaii, which sits atop an old volcano

and penetrates the heavens. Humility—
from the Latin *humilitas,* related to the adjective

humilis, meaning "humble" or "grounded,"
"from the earth." We send the dead

to their rooms without supper. We humiliate
them. Arrogance, meet anxiety. Anxiety,

meet Arrogance—quite the bickering couple.
Oedipus and Lear have nothing on me.

the guide

George Perreault

in the deep northern woods
when looking for a camp
you know is on a creek,

you should always plan to miss
either upstream or down,
so when finding that water

you'll know how to turn,
allowing deliberate error
to bring you safely home.

as the crow flies is hardly straight
but when we take to air there's always
a roundness to mind,

and engineers will tell you, even
though the Mackinac seems flat,
still they were pilots on a great circle.

the everyday might deceive you
into some flat hope you can carry
the world with ease,

but really, nowhere is up north, and
nowhere's down south; there's nothing
back east and nothing out west.

every journey has its own fullness,
each step taking you irretrievably further
over the rim of the world.

Moose

Lisa Fosmo

To honor you
We will burn a fire add copper
the hue of your coat
to make the many colors of spirit.
Then look for you in the lights
of the night sky,
in this trembling world
of mercury rising.

The hunters all cry wolf,
but the deer herd is strong.
Last year's fawns are plenty.

Yet this loss is thick.
The air becomes gravity gravy
when desolation seals fate.
A winter too warm
Is a perfect storm.
Thin ice becomes a trap.

To love something
is to surrender to it.
To bow to its weight.

Our grief is raw.
Two of our beloved moose
Float dead on the Lake.

The same moose that sauntered
our fields in summer, that swam
the lake behind our cabin,
while we watched in awe.

Part of the heard that loved
the pumpkins we left in fall.
These moose our neighbors,
all of them our beloveds.

Their once dark coat sun faded,
mammoth driftwood sculptures,
  fallen like toppled Trojan horses.

They've become an island hungry eagles visit.
  We go to pay homage one last time and witness
as these once earthly bound majestic giants
  soar the skies with eagles.

© Tom Barrat *American Bald Eagle at Walloon Lake* 2024

Grandpa's Gun

Scot Siegel

Retrieve it from a dry, dark place.
Pull it from a sleeve, some felt-like leather
with our name inscribed on a flimsy tag.
Examine it for any trace of him.

This was a gift to my father from his true father,
the one with spaniels and a hunting lodge,
not the one we could not speak of.
I take up the heft, and get the sense

I am looking down the long barrel of
some unknown history. He told me:
Safety-on, until you're absolutely ready.
Watch your stance; hold steady.

I scan the room. No window. No door.
Just the gun like an iron dove in my hand.
With love, I turn it over, brush my fingers across
the stock, find his initials in smooth silver ridges.

Turn over again, and drink from a spring called
The pooling of history, a chalice of blood, Chernihiv
forests at dusk… I have his chin, when I lift and pump
the muzzle; his shoulder when I place it in the crook,

his eyes pressing cold metal to my face.
Then his voice, when something faint
and terrible in the shape of my real name
burns through the cheekpiece.

Sublime

Caroline Helmstadt

There is something beyond,
out there in the wind.
Amidst the gentle birdsong and
crow caw,
sense it
taking shape.
Shifting and molding,
where
does it go?
The path
thick and tangled
by leaves softly stirring and
branches swaying this way
and that–
you,
relentless predator,
track it
for fear
you are lost.
Picking up momentum,
electricity coursing through your soul–
Be charged to realize
this:
You
were never lost–

this god
cannot be tracked
but only found
within.

© Caroline Helmstadt *Shadows of A Dream* 2024

The Northwoods

Jennifer Uehlein Reynolds

If you have never walked the northwoods in spring,
You may have missed red and green skunk cabbage heads,
Pointy ends making their way up out of
the swamp like an alien pod,
Or the whorl of the fiddlehead unfurling to become a fern.
You may not have tasted the garlicky onion
goodness of a wild leek in your potato soup,
Or seen a porcupine high in the tree branches,
looking for the first tender leaves at the
top where the sun hits first.
You may have missed the tiny tracks of the fawn
in the dirt, so delicate next to the doe's,
And the daffodils that signal the presence
of an old homestead site.

If you have never walked the northwoods in summer,
You may have missed the lush green tunnel of leaves,
The mossy pillows of emerald, and the
gnarled roots that surely house fairies.
The reflection of clouds over an unexpected lake,
Or the pleasure of cold stream water over your bare toes.
You may never have seen the pileated
woodpecker swoop through the trees,
Or heard the woosh of a raven's wings
as they echo between hills.

If you have not slept outside in the northwoods in summer,
You may have missed the shooting stars in
August, and the glow of the Milky Way.

If you have never walked the northwoods in fall,
You may have missed the vibrant red maple leaf that falls early,
Glowing on the trail amongst its less impressive brethren.
The bright yellow cap of the amanita mushroom,
reminiscent of Alice in Wonderland,
Or the ruffles of the Lion's Mane and Chicken of the Woods.
You may never have seen a valley of color stretch out
for miles, with no indication of civilization.
Or the salmon swimming upstream, occasionally
splashing like some prehistoric river monster.
You may have missed the wooly bear
caterpillar inching across the path,
its bands of black and rust brown indicating
the harshness of the winter to come.

If you have never walked the northwoods in winter,
You may have missed the tracks in the snow,
Of the creatures there that you almost never see, like the bobcat.
Or even the fat, plodding prints of a black bear, looking
for one last meal before curling up for its winter sleep.
Or the tiny prints of a mouse, or the
hieroglyphics of a flock of turkeys.
You may not have seen the black specks
of snow fleas on a sunny day,
Or the wing print in the snow of an owl who caught its prey.
If you have not slept in the northwoods in winter,
You may have missed the chortling of the great horned owl,

And the yip of coyotes as they close in on their prey,
Or the sound of falling snow, echoing in the stillness as it lands,
As you snuggle into your down quilt,
feeling as one with the universe.

These treasures are there,
If only you step out into the northwoods.

© Jennifer Uehlein Reynolds *Chapel Rock* 2024

Saturday Morning

Storm Ainsely

wake to steady rain
gentle windchime stirring
perch on porch stool to watch
stratus clouds soak rock lawn stark colors
my potted plants dripping & shiny
how they only look watered from the sky

I am slow with my morning coffee but
by the time I move to shower
I'm on the last cup in the pot
stratus breaking into stratocumulus outside
sun peeking through

my great-grandmother called those blue patches in between
sucker holes, as in, you're a sucker if you think that means
it's going to clear up
an apt observation for MI
In CA, where we rejoice over a tenth of an inch of rain
we have sucker clouds instead—
the dream of rain when it is not falling
the YouTube soundtrack for the classic pitter-patter

I let the tub fill as I shower & do the necessaries
it's been 5 days, so I wash my hair twice
turn water off & soak
holding my last cup of coffee gone cold

I watch soap swirls like clouds in the water
change to my subtle shifts underneath
cirrus patterns breaking around my knees
sticking out like mountains

Listen to neighbors getting home from an errand
locking beep & clatter drifting in open window
wonder if the clouds outside are already cumulus
or if we may have a cumulonimbus up there
hidden by the others—if we will get
the thunderstorms we have chances of

when the bathwater clouds fade from cirrus
to cirrocumulus to altostratus
it is time to get out,
there will be no sun haloes in my bathwater
just slowly appearing reflections of curtains & tap
pull the drain, shower back on to rinse
not yet thinking of how to get dressed
I know I'll search closet for clothes I rarely have
the temperatures to wear, rejoice in their coziness

go check on the clouds—still stratocumulus
shifting at once quickly & somehow lazily
taking their own time
maybe not sucker clouds today
we could yet get more rain
windchime clangs abruptly in agreement

Sunday Slow

Monique Bova

I took the morning Sunday slow
Letting the coffee steep
Grounds gently sinking to silt
As I tick-tucked pants into socks
A neighborhood amble reveals Nature's ambitious
Who started their day early
In the dusky
dripping
damp
Of yesterday's spatter
Presses of hoof and talon in the country corduroy
And also, here
And everywhere
Sticky languid lines traversing the gravel expanse-
Stalwart slugs
Trail their shimmery ribbons
Unraveling cloaks of liquid crystal
Impervious to sand and stone
Both

There was a summer
Thick and golden
Like Slow
In his muscled mantle
In his captured patch of garden
My son's fingers strung with slime
Holding the universe in a gallon pickle jar

And Slow
Former nemesis
His rasp-tongue ravishment
Of my vines and berries
Burned in my throat
Like the beer left to drown him
Now Slow
Cherished totem of boyhood wonder
Taught us from his windowed world
From his carved twists of tunnel
27,000 tongue-teeth
Ate his weight in kitchen cast-offs
Black beads telescoped
On their sticky stems
To voyeur back at us

But Slow
In solitary exile
Under a nail-pounded ceiling of stars
Followed his own tantalizing trail
To romance
Tin lid vent holes
Releasing remnant wafts of dill
And a midnight hoard of hermaphroditic miracles
Trailing their microscopic filaments
From jar to living room
To the dusky
dripping
damp
Of farmhouse basement
Progeny found for years to come
Pilfering from the cat bowl

So Slow
Wends his sticky languid legacy
Into my Sunday thoughts
Knees gently sinking to sand
Denim press on the country corduroy
And also, here
And everywhere
Curious tentacles taste the morning
I taste it too
In warm sips to birdsong
Remembering how Isaac Watt
Called me a worm
In my Sunday morning childhood pew
Like it was a bad thing
Like god would avert his eyes from
These humble wonders
Collectively crossing the expanse
On this celestial patch of garden
Impervious to shame and damnation
Both

Morning Boat on Walloon

Margaret Anderson

Let me tell you what I remember
about fishing with my father
in the morning fog on Walloon,
our oars silent as a mink paddling,
to catch breakfast in Lily Pad Bay:

his face, with its gray vacation beard,
relaxed beneath the frayed brim of his cap,
his fingers exploring the dirt
in a foam cup of Walt's Crawlers
bought from a blind man
at a roadside stand
along Boyne City Road;

bait on, his easy cast and a sigh
from us both as we settled in
for the wait, for the nibble, for the reel-in,
skimming with the dragonflies,
absorbing the dawning sunlight like reeds
among the shallows, thinking only that
now was the best now for a fish.

I recall the smell of waterlogged birch
and moments of peace
which rose like bubbles from the silt —
his call to a robin, his recitation of Longfellow,
his whistled tunes echoing the forest primeval,
and our respite among the lily pads.

© Taylor Keiser *Place for Rest* 2024

Like July

Patty Durell

Every swim is holy but some swims are proof of divinity. Divinity like the sun, not like confessionals. Like Bible Beach on Bois Blanc Island. Like forgiveness without pleading. Like Sciamma's *Do all lovers feel like they're inventing something?* Like adding Lou Reed's *Perfect Day* to what is supposed to be a happy playlist. Like how I've unexpectedly seen the northern lights twice in Cheboygan while some people search their whole lives with no such luck. Like the first cold day when the last snowbird has fled and town gently rearranges itself to hold those who stay, tucking the corners in and pushing us all a little closer to the center. Like how summer starts to shorten the day after it finally, selfishly begins. Like how the edge of the earth is a roadside beach twenty minutes west of the Mackinac bridge. Like how toddlers and pets both innately know bad attention is still attention, and adults forget attention is a perfectly fine thing to want. Like really, really wanting something. Like how I wonder if I drive eighty minutes round trip to the Harbor Springs pool every week because it feels good or because it makes me Good. Like how this is my third summer swimming every day and I still don't have a method for getting itchy sand out of my shower, my shoes, my beach sandwiches, my ungrateful complaints. Like trying to forget the mistake of googling pictures of sea lampreys. Like bathing in light. Like baptisms in Great Lakes. Like the welcomed silence underwater after jumping off Petoskey's break wall. Like my therapist asking, "Where do you feel that in your body?" and just guessing. Like neither of you letting go even when your hands start to get clammy. Like how sometimes I want a car to cut me off in traffic so I can feel justified in my anger, honk loudly with an audience witnessing my hounding. Like that one blazing week you let yourself believe Lake Superior feels warm. Like telling time from a Lake Michigan sunset. Like how Lake Huron feels like a secret the more north you drive. Like the sweetness of reading something you know they'd like chased by the bitterness of knowing you won't be telling them. Like waiting for the less popular blue hour that follows the showy golden one. Like how during the dog days, I suddenly don't mind the sticky cost of a twist dipped in sprinkles dripping down my freckled arm. Like black flies biting you at Presque Isle. Like the initial shock of learning something disguised as a common house fly can sting so bad. Like wondering if they show the songs you introduced to them to someone else, and if they pay the pricey toll that is silently remembering it was you first. Like wondering if that matters. Like deciding it doesn't but hoping for it anyways. Like how a humid summer sleep is a badge of honor and bad mouthing air conditioning is a northern right. Like the ache of an overdue laugh with your friend declaring that nothing has been that funny in a long time. Like believing them. Like acne scars. Like stretch marks. Like the age spot on my twenty seven year old left hand that only shows up in July. Like July. Like swimming in northern Michigan in July.

Tomatoes in August

Patty Durell

I've never been rich but I have had tomatoes in August
August waits for me
It holds the door, stops while I tie my shoes
Points at the calendar promising *we have plenty of time*

If June tastes like a Blood Orange Honey on draft
And July a sickly sweet cherry
August is a five hour breakfast
Unannounced in its arrival but indulgent in its honesty

I waste time by counting it
I say goodbye to Lake Huron three days in a row
Achingly slow in my surrender to an end
Foolish to have hoped it would've liked to linger longer, for me

My tongue is evidence of change
I'm seasoned in using my back molars
To rip eagerly into delicate grape tomatoes
Betraying the taste of my younger self

I leave teeth marks on sun soaked heirlooms
And fingerprints on all you'll remember
I leave in early hours without waking anyone
As a cruel and loving act of preservation

Loosening my grip, I look down stunned
Hands empty and out of breath from holding on
I'd pridefully suffer for more August days
But August would never ask that of me

I've never forgotten but I have had tomato toast, salted
While I try to forgive August
For August is a liar
I'm desperate to believe

When there is nothing left to let go of
Once my final fit of refusal is thrown
After I've begged despite vowing to restrain
I'm reminded how much I love Autumn

on the nature of eaton street

-in memory of Mary Cook

Sheri Green

i did not have cakes and butter
a jar of jam
a sandwich nor an apple
when i huffed up self's hill
to the empty lots on eaton street
with mother's garden shears
and a mason jar
to cut blue chicory
queen anne's lace
and pink everlasting pea–
there were no sweets nor wine
nor a red velvet wrap
as i skipped along the path
into rows of red pine
darted to your side door
rang the bell
left my tussie-mussie
–as you phrased it–
and dashed to touch my
pale shoulder to the far side
of a towering red-brown trunk
until i heard   yoo-hoo
and my name
and i ran to your outstretched arms
to ask how you knew–
you snorted that i was a wisp

not a trickster in disguise
as you stepped inside
to put the mason-jar-posy
on your fieldstone hearth–
then returned to sit with me in woven chairs
where we donned brimmed hats
sprinkled with peanuts and sunflower seeds
and as patient as statues
we waited for chickadees

The Old Men (of Mackinac) are Gone

Jim Bolone

No pedigree or briefcase
Or calling card;
Only calloused hands,
Worn soles,
And fervor for life
With shoulders once broad,
Jawlines resolute,
Carving dreams against time.

Look about Mackinac,
Observe their results —
No swan song for them,
Theirs plays in the memories of those who know,
Who relish in the wake of splendor.

The old men are gone now.
What will we do.

Glacial Till

Jeanne Blum Lesinski

After seven decades, the farmhouse where our mother spent her teenage years in northern Michigan thaws. Thaws from the contentious sibling ownership and the gradual blight of our mother's Alzheimer's. Uncle had portrayed his taking over responsibility for the farm on behalf of our mother as a gift to us eventual inheritors, but his insistence that everything in the house remain frozen in time has hardly been generous--certainly not to me, the only person living close enough to the property to use it much.

When I realized that I'd long had as much legal right as Uncle to use the property but been tricked into thinking otherwise, anger flared. I admit that during the eight years Mom disintegrated, I was struggling to dig out from an avalanche in my own life. I'd had little energy to claim the right and with it the tasks needed to make the 1958 house habitable.

The situation changed after Mom's estate was finally settled. When we siblings relinquished our interest in the property to our youngest sibling Todd, he promised each of us access to the property. A piece of Northern Michigan, a landing pad for adventures at the tip of the mitt.

In May three of us siblings and a friend gather to clean the house, so that in July we can have a family reunion, the first since our mother's funeral five years earlier. It's hard to know where to start but collecting desiccated mice and taking the shop vac to the flies and Asian beetles from upstairs to the basement seem as good as any.

In the fieldstone and cement basement the clutter and the filth almost paralyze us, but Todd is a powerhouse of industriousness. We condense the contents of mildewed boxes into newer boxes and haul the old ones to the fire pit behind the pump house. Once Todd charges up the stairs with a box of quilting squares and a family of mice that he throws onto the lawn.

Two white chest freezers are a focal point. One is empty with the lid propped open. The other, a Norge big enough to hold a butchered deer, is still running. Todd and I look at each other. Wide-eyed, we giggle at whatever our imaginations have conjured as the freezer contents. I think that Uncle might just fit inside but see my mother's disapproving face.

When their mother died, four siblings inherited the farm on twenty acres. Uncle wanted to buy out the other siblings' shares but didn't have the money, so he'd talked Mom into going in with him to buy them out. Though she wasn't all that interested in the farm, he was her younger brother and he'd managed to persuade her somehow. They'd set up a tenant in common ownership deal. I wonder if Mom knew then that this nebulous legal structure of equal ownership rights might spell trouble. She'd held her ground against extravagant expenses Uncle had wanted her to fund. She couldn't hold her ground against Alzheimer's.

"How much do you think the electric bill is," I ask Todd.

"No way to know," he says. "The electric co-op won't tell me anything because the bill is in Uncle's name, and he's been paying it all these years. He's not telling me much, but I've told him I have to know stuff if he expects me to help pay upkeep."

"Or improvements--except he doesn't want any."

"Don't worry," says Todd. "It's fifty-fifty. I have just as much right to make decisions as he does."

"You know, I would've come here sometimes. I live in a one-bedroom apartment in the city," I say, moving filthy cloth rags and a basket of clothes pins from the top of the Norge. "I could've used a break. But I never felt welcome because he's accused everyone of stealing things, like things that Mom took downstate when Grandmother was living with her those last years. Ugh."

Jim, the farmer down the road who has been harvesting hay from the fields since Grandmother was alive and knew our mother too, had become a sort of caretaker. He'd helped get a natural gas boiler installed to replace the propane furnace. He'd had the 1958 well pump fixed time and again. He'd insisted that the elms that grew up where the fuel tank once stood be sawed down before they took out the cinderblock wall of the back room where the milk from the cows was processed. The roots had already gotten a good start.

"Jim says that Uncle hasn't been here in over ten years," I say.

"What's the likelihood that he's going to show up anytime soon?"

We shrug.

After Todd decides to unplug the freezer, we return to the dead insects while we await the thaw. I'm happy to be interrupted by a voice from above announcing that some friends have arrived. I climb the stairs with its pair of worn boots resting on the left of each step. Noting the one replaced board, raw wood unlike the dark green painted ones, the memory of a slip and fall on these stairs as a teenager flits through my mind. This place is so full of memories that it's hard to shovel through them, let alone dig out of them. Yet, this realization pangs when I think of my mother and all the memories that melted away in her decay.

I welcome my former teaching colleague and her husband and their three grade-school boys into the living room. They've just come from a pizza joint and will soon head back to their mostly off-the-grid cabin some dozen miles north to finish their long weekend. Even though we haven't seen each other since before the pandemic hit, the hugs are big and the smiles are bigger. We shoo the guys outside so we can catch up with the highlights, that include her promotion and work on a Ph.D. An hour later we make promises to get together on their pontoon boat someday, and they are off.

Then Todd and I go at the glacier inside the Norge, he with a knife, prying out the ice and the items lost inside. We fill a white speckled, black metal canner pot with ice that I carry outside and dump near a hydrangea. At the Norge, I open the wide mouth of the black contractor's bag. Into it go yellow plastic tubs with black grease pen inscriptions or masking tape labels on which Grandmother had indicated the contents and date in the perfect Palmer penmanship of solo teacher in the one-room schoolhouse where she'd worked when she'd met our widowed future grandfather.

I pull out a block covered in a plastic wrapper, brush away the snow to find the pale blue rose cake topper from Grandfather's eighty-fifth birthday party (he was born in 1891). Holding it transports me back to the party in the simple township hall that, directed by our mother and grandmother, we'd helped clean and decorate with white tablecloths, blue crepe paper streamers, and vases of wildflowers. My brother remembers it was he who'd picked the Queen Anne's Lace and black-eyed-Susans. Mom's down South younger brother had brought a box of pecans, and we kids had played with the strangers we'd maybe met once before, if we were old enough to remember our cousins before they'd moved South. Finally, back in the present, I reverentially lower the cake from 1976 into the black bag.

"Swiss chard, 1974!"

"1972!"

It's become a kind of contest to see how low in the freezer and back in time we can go. The exploded home-canned goods we see on the back basement shelf make us think that time travel is possible.

"1969!"

I telescope back in memory to '69 and the realization that I was then eight years old and well sheltered from the tumultuous events of the time. The Viet Nam War. The Civil Rights movement. Dad saying that when teaching at a high school on 12 Mile, he could see the smoke from protest fires burning Detroit. I'm frozen there because I cannot remember this house from a younger viewpoint. I've gotten to the core of my memory of the farm, but not to a solid place in my feelings about the contentious situation.

Then I think of how curious, how social Grandmother always was. She'd been a member of the church community, a product tester for some state home ec organization, a researcher into family genealogy. Always a teacher, always a learner. She'd never have wanted her home to become a mausoleum. I envision the ice cracking on the Pigeon River in spring. Instead of the fire crackle at the rubbish burning hoop, I hear the sound of moving water, like laughter, and see smiles around a campfire.

Later that afternoon, Todd and I take a plastic bag of thawed dehydrated morels to the edge of the hayfield. Hoping some spores might be viable, we scatter them under a wild apple tree.

© Nancy Hayes *Omena Bay* 2024

Unto This World

J. L. Hagen

Unto
    this world,
        we come
            one way,
       desire's
          consequence;

             And leave behind,
        when journey's done
    but remembering,
          unprecedence.

             In between,
      a word we give
          to earth and sky and sea,
      and like Superior's
          heaving sigh,
             breathe life
          into a soul
      or two
      or three;

Then, to a loneliness return,
    like salmon tumbled down
         a leaf-strewn stream;

No further thoughts
            or words or deeds,
         but memory's hunger
     for a fading dream

   Of future lives yet unconceived,
               for whom a universe or two await;
               of unimagined things unnamed
                     and undone deeds
         thoughts uncontemplate.

   Dry ache, low now
on a bitter wind,
flowing into reverie's end,
      which, in its rush to fill the void,
         spins spring-fresh breezes 'round river's bend.

Hitchhiking Up North

Deborah Hochberg

Setting off to hitchhike
     from Detroit to northern Michigan
  in my 19th year
     standing out along the highway
delivering ourselves to chance, to kismet
   long shadeless stretches
     with the August sun beating down

I didn't quite admit it
     at the time, but I was
starting to wonder how
     I let you talk me into this

Such innocence and naïveté
     getting into whichever vehicle
  stopped for us
without a thought
   it could lead to our last day

Like getting in the cab
     with the two truckers
  from Tennessee
     so glad you were there
  to make conversation

And the man
        who picked us up
    outside of Bay City
  and let us camp for the night
        in his backyard
      where we saw the northern lights

Throwing ourselves into the world
        like so much flotsam
        living the American dream
            of footlooseness
        being on the move
            and on the road
    on the I-75 corridor
        two pilgrims traveling north

That was the end
        of our summer in Ann Arbor
    we knew we would never return
        to the house on Oak Street
            and that we would be changed

Picking blueberries near the shore of Lake Michigan
            huddled in a tent through a violent storm
        getting lost on a wilderness trail
            a kindly ranger picking us up
        and delivering us back to the road
            to resume our rambles

Finally reaching
     your old neighbor's campground
  on the shore of a lake
     whose name I no longer remember

At some point in time
     sleeping on the ground
  with nothing but a flimsy nylon bag
      between me and the elements
  completely lost its appeal

But back then, in the morning
     frying cornbread with blueberries
  in a cast iron pan
    over a campfire
 we knew we were doing
     what it was we wanted to do
 living out some kind of shared
    dream of paradise
      inhabiting our own private Eden

if only

Sheri Greene

so fast so fast–
a jagged flash lit the blackened horizon
cleaving the bruised sky
then searing shut like a cauterized wound

if only our wipers would shear off
fly past
force a pull over
provide an excuse to tumble out
and race across the sand
whooping into the roar of thunder and wave
brazen under the lacerated sky

if only–
soaked in the deluge
soused in adrenaline
and scoured clean–
we could with impeccable timing leap into the rent
then land hard and whole and alive
our skin tingling
the taste of copper in our mouths
our wounds sealed shut

Lake Effect

Scot Siegel

The night wind unwinds
rousing our neighbors' voices;
the heatwave breaking.

Remember the lake?
Stars swarmed like caddisflies
kissing the surface.

The wind did not sleep
moving endlessly between
overheated rooms

of birch and pine,
seeking schist or granite slab;
a place to lie down.

Let's find that relief
slip into bathymetric daze
let the breeze barter

uncharted stars for
night swimmers, far from the dock —
let minnows caress our toes.

© Scot Siegel *Kleber Pond* 2024

Just Like That

John Lennon

I am strung up like porch lights
Lost in the glare of the sun lingering
Along the shoreline, between sullen homes.
And just like that, summer is over.

Tight against September,
Some might wish to go back,
But I press my nose down to the first fallen leaves
As they whisper the possibility of quiet streets
Where lovers used to walk on more tepid evenings.

At times, the harbor clock strikes the hour,
But I know it is late
By the honeyed amber air
And the gloaming of the sky.

Late Iosco Autumn (a haiku)

Hank Kaufmann

Killing frosts at night
Rutting whitetails in dim light
Blood Red Berry Leaves.

November Witch

Julie Angeli

Popular name for the frequent and brutal system of windy storms that come screaming across the Great Lakes from Canada every autumn – Farmer's Almanac

The witch storms in after
the falling leaves
her winds strong
her gales stronger

Stirs her cauldron
under the frost moon
rocking the inland sea
sending creatures into the deep

Paints slate-colored breakers
with white caps and rain
waves tumble and roll
tossing freighters

Sends her storms
a warning mariners best heed
lest they find early graves
in the frigid depths

Her spell complete
when the winter ice calms
while Superior sleeps
dreaming of spring

© Elizabeth M. Bates *Crow Over Lake Superior* 2024

Second Nature

David James "DJ" Savarese

Caught basking in the sun,
The young maple blushes:

September's understudy,
rehearsing loss.

She's all soliloquy,
this leafy Ophelia.

Beneath the sycamore,
squirrels bury nuts,

salvage what's left
of summer.

The fire's embers,
nothing now but ash,

haunt the old stone hearth.
The chatter around it—

as if declaimed--
turns iambic.

Upon Watching the Moon Move

Ellen Schettling Whitehead

Taking just ten minutes
to watch the moon
slowly make its way
from one jagged tree edge
to its opposite side

I sat in silent wonder

Glimpses of its bright glow
changed into intricate shapes
as the moon moved along
amongst black branches
brushing the orb softly

Never having taken the time
to actually see the moon move
I was awestruck

I know that science tells me
the moon circles earth
the earth circles sun
forever and always

But what I did not know
was how holy
ten minutes
can be

blue black nights

Carrie Cantalupo

follow these smoked days
soot smeared sunsets
over gray Lake Michigan

the realization
that today's walk
was weighted by distant fires
out of control
climate that brings
to the woods
slow animation of squirrels
the hazy float of butterflies
swallow tail over the milkweed
droop of leaves
no wind
just heavy
heavy air

sumac

Carrie Cantalupo

we whacked the sumac
dragged it to the brush pile
angry branches tangled
grabbing at us till we could burn it
a battle we never seemed to win

inevitably new rhizomes
pushed themselves defiantly
throughout the yard
standing their ground
in the vegetables and flower beds

resorting to research
consulting landscapers
we sharpened shears
bought sharp shovels
prepared for true warfare

then learning
sumac's familial ties to cashews
their flowers used for spicy teas
or beautiful burgundy dyes
homeopathic medicinal extracts

dissections of the buds and berries
the blossoms lemony tang
velvety staghorns with
leaves that curl and change
color with the seasons

now we let them
burgeon on the fringe of the woods
dramatic craggy branches that nod
their red tasseled heads reminding us
sometimes our enemies are really friends

Rhyme and Reason: a Northern Michigan Love Story in the time of Pandemic

Monique Bova

The world told us that distance was love
And in the absence of embrace
we sat shoulder to shoulder
Perched on the dunes as the sun slid
slightly more than strangers
You told me whales sometimes come
right up on the Vancouver shore
to scratch themselves against the rocks
How wonderful it must feel, I thought
the pebble's edge on those untouched places
You said you cried when you saw it
moved by their magnitude
And I heard it then-
a shared song

The world told us to hold our breath
But in the novelty of nearness
we laid face to face
Languidly defiant
on a bed of moss
The April sun pouring over us
effervescent like the beer
you pulled out of the backpack
What do you taste, you asked me
over the edge of the cup
I leaned in to kiss you

Your lips were warm and new
What do you taste, I asked myself-
Something brewing?

The world told us there was no harm in hiding
And in the pain of previous disappointments
we squared off heartache to heartache
Sprawled across a sandy sheet
on Second Beach
the sun as unrelenting
as your magic-fingered card cutting
No need for a cribbage board to remind us
it was time to make the next move
But what do you want, you asked
The question as bewildering
as an unforeseen forfeit
We survived that silent hiding season
like a seed survives the suffocating press of snow
Stratified in dormancy
and a necessary waiting
for the beach beams of another summer
to breach our protective layers
And your soft-eyed smile over a six-card deal
sighed the first notes of a building crescendo
The answer sprouting then
a tender tentative stem of possibility
This, I smiled back-
You

Perhaps the world wasn't expecting us
to build a bridge of words
across mandated solitude

But amidst the throbbing hush
of that collective hunker
we met in the middle
each with our storied burdens
to find ourselves holding the same end
on a string of chance encounters
Both startled and delighted
Like finding a rock in the crook of a tree branch
and wondering by what chance
it came to be there

Perhaps the world tried to deafen us
with its breaking waves of global panic
pounding in our ears
like a hateful metronome
But instead
while the whippoorwill called its brazen love into the darkness
we sang our own careful song
A rustic rubato
lapping its irregular rhythm
along the sunset margins of the beaver bottom
Nudge of wind
and tug of bank
making time where time was needed
Both intentional and accidental
Like a caddis gathering up the scattered pieces
and wondering by what chance
it suddenly came to be home

In a world that demanded we adhere to the map
We explored instead in concentric circles
Following the river's meander

and allowing ourselves to hope
that eventually we would get there
Like an ancient aquifer
wending its way through that stony hold
to fresh freedom in a forest bowl
You're my girl, you say
as we shed our clothes
and slip into the mysterious turquoise
Welcome home, I say
as we shed our clothes
and slip beneath the top sheet
I find the curl of your body
Long Macedonian thighs and lips now
warm and familiar
My belly soft and shaped like pasta and happiness
And the slow simmering Sunday sauce
you hold out on the spoon for me to try
What does it need, you ask
Both savory and sweet
Just a little more time, I think-
and this could be perfect

Now we settle to sleep as the sun slides
so much more than lovers
The sounds of the swamp pouring over us
crisp and delicious
like the well-water you bring me in a mason jar
I like it here, you whisper
to that goosebump spot behind my ear
And I cry when I hear it
Moved by its magnitude
A sound as familiar as our creaky front door

as clear as the midnight elk bugle
and as distinct as the dusky gulp of a feeding trout
Wending its way through our stony holds
Awe and gratitude like the pebble's
edge on our untouched places
Thrumming with both rhyme and reason
I hear it still-
our song

© Taylor Keiser *Road to Peace* 2024

Bumblebee Kisses

Katherine Foote

I'm sorry miss, for
Bumping into you
I was looking for flowers,
Some nectar and pollen but
I appreciate
You letting me bee

**CROOKED TREE ARTS CENTER
YOUNG WRITERS EXPOSITION
2023 FIRST PLACE WINNERS**

First Place Poetry-Elementary

"Bob the Dog" by Shain Mahaney
St. Francis Xavier School, 5th Grade

I am a golden, swift and playful dog,
Who sat on a dirty, bug filled log.
I take a walk with my master every day,
He wants to walk but I want to play.

I'm friends with a snorty, brown, hilarious hog,
I'm also friends with an old, jolly, massive bulldog.
I like to eat cookies and tasty ice cream,
I'm on the brand new puppy bowl team.
One thing I don't like is gigantic planes,
My friends always ride amusing looking trains.

One day we went to a relatively little park,
When I went to make a cheerful, loud bark.
Trevor, my owner, went on this thing,
I remember him telling me it is a swing.

After he finished took me home,
Then he brushed me with a brown, soft comb.
I love my owner, Trevor,
And he loves me.
I'll stay with him forever,
Until I have to pee.

"Stuck in a Pyramid" by Lillian Berry
St. Francis Xavier School, 5th Grade

Uly was afraid. He pressed his boot into the sand. The hot sun shone onto him as the warm wind circled him. He found his courage and let his feet guide him into the pyramid.

He was currently in a…some would call it a vacation. He called it a business trip. Well, it really WAS. He had a job with his sister. It was this extraordinary trip that Uly was not excited for . Uly and his sister Abby were the stars of their own TV show entitled Treasure-Hunters. This was their first episode. Uly was really just there to hold and angle the camera right.

Originally, this was Abby's idea. Uly had said "No" to it then. "C'mon!" Abigail was already heading deeper into the torch-lit passage. She swiveled around the corner and vanished from sight. Uly knew she was still there, but he scampered over to her, almost tripping. He felt cornered. Trapped. Stuck. The walls were so close together… the tiles felt uncomfortable on his feet, even with boots on! Uly gulped. Abby scoffed and mumbled to herself. Finally, she spoke aloud. "Uly, we HAVE to do this! You agreed to it." He did agree. Abby turned another sharp corner.

"Wait up!" he called, starting to feel dreadful. No answer came. He picked up his feet and started around the corner. No Abby, either. He KNEW something WAS GOING TO GO WRONG. "ABBY!" his voice echoed against the tomb-like walls. He took another step, but his boot never hit the ground.

Uly tripped forward before he had any time to look down. He fell into a small, narrow chamber. "Uly!" Uly lifted his head and looked straight into Abby's glowing face after he'd landed.

He would've probably smiled but the fact that they were in a sandstone cage prevented that.

"You shouldn't walk so slow!" she pointed out. "You shouldn't run ahead! Look, now we're stuck. No one's gonna find us, and we've no water or food. I'm sure we're going to DIE!" he shouted, despite his fear of the dark. Suddenly Abby's face wasn't smiling anymore. She wasn't even looking at him. Well, it was in the same direction, he thought so, but it was very hard to tell in the dark. "Uly…" her voice trailed off as torches' flames suddenly flickered out of them.

Uly blinked several times and turned around. They weren't in a cage—there were no bars at all. What stood before him were giant golden pillars, and many other riches such as goblets with embedded jewels and golden plates with hieroglyphs. "WE'RE RICH!" Abby threw out her arms and swung around the pillars. Uly was the type of person who always saw the bad side of situations. For example: the crumbling bricks on the wall opposite of him didn't look promising. The rocks continued to fall until finally the wall broke apart. It was like the wall simply had shrunk into itself. Of course, Abby hadn't noticed, she was currently trying to bury herself in gold, but Uly obviously had. There was a shadow that looked as if it had a dog's head and a human body.

"Ohmylittlesnuggiebugs," the shadow said very hastily in a babying kind of voice. Suddenly Abby noticed and jumped up. Gold sprang from every corner. The shadow yelped and peered its head out of the passageway. It was a very surprised looking Egyptian dog head. "Visitors!" it said. "It's been so very long since I had visitors." It then stalked out and looked at them. It was holding a mummified cat who was ALIVE. "Aren't you going to bow or at least kneel to me?" Abby had noticed its pet, too. "What is THAT? Is it alive? Can it talk? Who are you? How is your costume headpiece moving its mouth when you speak? Why should we bow?" She pestered him with questions.

"ENOUGH," it finally said instead of answering. "I am the pharaoh, mighty and powerful. THAT'S why you should bow. This is my familiar, Dune." It nodded its long snout at the cat. "It is VERY MUCH ALIVE."

"If you're the pharaoh… What's your name?"

"Hapshetsut."

Nice name, Uly silently thought to himself as Abby asked more questions. "Can we just call you Hap? It's a lot easier." The pharaoh sighed, then Abby picked out another question. "Hey! If that's just a mask how does it make, like, facial expressions? Like sighing, or squinting?" Then the mask became angry looking.

"It's ENCHANTED OK!?"

Abby ducked and hastily spoke, "Okay, okay." That's when Uly broke in. "Wait. How do we get out of here? I mean, no offense, I don't want to… end up like you." He looked at Hap. "Oh. There is no way out. I mean, this was all made for me. Why would I want to leave?" He tilted his dog mask.

"No. Way. OUT?!" Uly gasped and Abby suddenly darted out of sight. Uly turned around and watched Abby grab hordes of golden items. "Are you gonna help me OR NOT?!" she shouted at him and struggled lifting the heavy gold. She plopped it into a pile underneath the passage that went up to the surface. Uly realized her plan and rushed over to help her. In a minute or two the siblings stood beside each other, panting in the sweltering heat. A tower of golden plates and other items stood in front of them, leading up to their escape. Abby scurried up quickly and leaped up onto the top. She got out. Uly nodded his head at the pharaoh who yawned and clambered up behind. He jumped up and succeeded like Abby. Uly ran out, sunlight dazzling him.

"Did you get that?" Abby asked, her eyes shining. And to Uly's surprise, he DID get that. "Now to our next show." Abby looked out across the horizon.

First Place Poetry-Middle School

"The Woes of a Euphonium Player" by Owen Saunders
Petoskey Middle School, 7th Grade

The euphonium player stands alone
Beneath the spotlight's golden tone
A silent giant in the band
Whose woes are hard to understand

With a heavy heart and mellow sound
The euphonium's notes resound
But often lost in the mix
Overlooked by flashy tricks

The trumpets roar and trombones blaze
While the euphonium player stays
Playing steady, strong, and true
But rarely noticed for all they do

Their fingers dance across the keys
Creating music with ease
But the world still fails to see
The beauty of their melody
But now the tone begins to shift
As inspiration takes a lift
For in this moment, I must say
An ode is what I wish to play

Oh, Euphonium, how wondrous your sound
A brass instrument that truly astounds
With a range so vast and a tone so sweet
Your music lifts us up on wings to greet

Your sound is like velvet, soft and sublime
A rare beauty that stands the test of time
From the heights of joy to the depths of sorrow
Your music glides us to a brighter tomorrow

In the hands of a master, you are a king
A regal instrument that makes our hearts sing
With passion and skill, your music takes flight
And fills our soul with a beautiful light

So, here's to you, euphonium
The way your music opens doors
A true treasure of the brass band
And a joy to all who take your hand

Even though you are forgotten
I remember you
And hope that your wonderful tone
Will soon again be shown

"A Fearful Encounter" by Zane Parish
Charlevoix Middle/High School, 8th Grade

Pvt. Hugh McNeal, Montana July 15, 1806

I am writing this in haste, for a fearful encounter runs laps through my mind. And though I struggle to finger through the terror laden rubble that fills my head, nothing but the memory of my visitors' shining amber eyes comes to show.

Before I met the beast, I was traveling alone on horseback, when I had foolishly been stalled by a glorious view. The mountains, vast in size, shone brightly in the sunlight. However, unbeknownst to me, a large, black beast drew nearer from the bushes.

Towering in size, the beast revealed itself as a bear by rising up on its hind legs and letting out a blood curdling growl. Overwhelmed and powerless, my cowardly horse threw me from its saddle, landing me beneath the bear's scruffy chin; its putrid breath warm upon my face.

The bear raised itself again, posturing to take a blow at my feeble body. Without thinking, I quickly grabbed my gun and set it upright below the wild beast's chest.

Having fallen on the tip of my rifle, the bear was stunned, but not for long. I took this opportunity to search for my gun. Upon finding it, I was disappointed to see that my rifle had been bent causing trepidation to ripple down my spine.

Hurriedly, I found my way up some sturdy branches and hid within the security of a nearby tree. I must have crawled like a madman, as I can still feel the rough bark tearing against my pants.

Feeling safe up in the tree, I cursed at the bear, mocking its incompetent display under my breath. Maybe its claws were just too blunt. For when it tried to climb the smooth trunk, it slipped. Snarling at its own pitiful failure, the beast glared up at me with those shining amber eyes.

As I wearily waited in the tree, I contemplated my situation. If I had only known, following my departure from St. Louis, that this journey would have me undergo such an enthralling encounter with death, perhaps I would have had more misgivings about the long journey. The sole purpose of this expedition relied on Jefferson's interest in exploring the Louisiana Territory and to locate a trade route to the Pacific Ocean. We set out from St. Louis, a small town located near the eastern outskirts of Missouri and continued traveling west across the Louisiana Territory which was our final destination. At last, resting at the Pacific Northwest, I took in its expansive shorelines, grateful to have made it that far.

But how things had changed since then, for by this part of the journey, I had found myself sitting in a tree, licking dry lips, half asleep and malnourished. Slowly opening my eyes, I shivered as I looked out at the dark chilling night. Suddenly reminded of the bear, I sat up and peaked into the blanketing twilight below. I found nothing but my broken gun, shining within the light of the moon. Glad the bear had departed, I cautiously descended the tree and arrived at camp in good health.

In the end, I am relieved to have escaped that beast, with its shining amber eyes, for if God is gracious, I will witness the expansion of the United States. I believe this expedition will truly set America towards the future, as we have made several bonds with Native American tribes who seek out trade. And now that I am safe at camp, I can get back to serving my country and exploring this beautiful land.

First Place Poetry- High School

"Rebound" by MaKayla Ramsay
Harbor Springs High School, 10th Grade

The world as we know it has come crashing down,
But not in the way where we ever hear its sound.
Where has the innocence in our children gone?
When did cursing and slurs leave our system redrawn?
What happened to having conversations with friends?
When did we decide that Snapchat was the trend?
Historic events that could have helped save,
Still led society to fall, to misbehave.
It's a terrifying fact when you stop and think,
That our planet, as we know it, is nearing its brink.
Students scream as they hear the dreadful sound,
One so recurrent, of shots heard round.
When did such horror become the new norm?
So much controversy, so much to transform.
Social media has left us divided,
Why can't we see that its content is one-sided?
What happened to our nation joining together as one?
When did political parties and fake news leave us all in stun?
Our approaching downfall is ever so discreet,
But if we do not make a change, the annihilation will complete.
Everyday people mindlessly check their phones,
To the point where AI could make us all clones.
A lack of employees is leaving our economy hurting,
It won't be much longer until this habit is alerting.
Why do we side and say people are wrong?
Instead of striving to simply get along.
When did the youth see a rise in their flaws?

Why is their faultless skin slashed from an unknown cause?
How did photoshopped models engrave our brains?
To the point of loved ones stuck with remains.
I say this to everyone in hope of a change,
Let us not see one another as inferior or strange.
We're all players of an identical game,
So should we individually be placing the blame?
Our world as we know it is slowly crashing down,
United, as one, we can make it rebound.

"Late Spring" by Rachael Rosenthal
Harbor Light Christian School, 11th Grade

The morning sun flickered through each crack of the blinds, until all stripes of light adorned the poster-scattered walls of Oswald's apartment. He awoke with a weak groan and turned over in his bed, squinting to see the blur of numbers on his alarm clock.

The sun has started to rise early again, to accompany the recent welcoming of spring. It's been making him wake up before his alarm. There are worse things to be irritated by, but it was the little things that got to him lately. Like how even little matches can add together to start large fires.

Oswald sat up and stared at the floor. He ran his fingers through his straight auburn hair, bangs falling back to cover his eyes. No thoughts ran through his head at this hour. Well, maybe one—one thought that had a secret passageway that led to a spiral staircase of other thoughts, woes, ideas—he hated change.

He hated when the seasons and weather changed. Even with a slow transition, he felt he couldn't keep up. He detested when people came and went, when feelings come and go. He didn't particularly like how most things in life were temporary. He couldn't handle it at times.

Even now, it's spring, and the world around him has been altered. Again.

Oswald stumbled out of bed, caring enough to throw on a decent outfit and clean himself up a bit. He grabbed his messenger bag and opened the front door of his apartment, turning back to eye the narrow hallway. A small window looked back at him. The morning sun had crawled in with perfect timing to reach his skin.

He remembered his waking resentment and scoffed, slamming the door behind him and rushing to the stairwell.

Oswald bounced down the front steps of his apartment complex, halting to take a deep breath of the fresh spring air. There was a light breeze, gently rustling the budding branches of trees, guiding cheerful birds through the air, brushing stray hairs to tickle his cheeks. It was a fight to stay moody now.

Bicycles ringed by, individuals and their dogs passed as Oswald headed to a nearby café, where colleagues had invited him to join them for a light breakfast. In honesty, only one had invited him, assuring him through his nervous refusal and reminders of social anxiety that it would be, to say the most, tolerable. The colleague had said straightforwardly that Oswald needed to get out more; he tended to shut himself in when he felt down and under the weather.

And now, facing the weather, he stood in front of the café, hesitating to go in. As a breeze carrying the scent of blooming flowers made him sneeze, he heard a familiar voice call his name. He had been spotted; the acquainted group had chosen to sit outside. Oswald stared down at his shoes as he walked over and braced introductions.

He patiently sipped at a hot coffee, raising a brow in surprise of how friendly everyone was to him, how welcomed he felt. This same morning he wanted to dig a hole and hide at the thought of everyone and everything outside of his comfort zone.

He glanced at his familiar colleague, who was amid a humorous conversation with another, but locked eyes with him. The man paused and shot an idiotic grin.

Oswald couldn't help but smile back, the sun casting a spotlight on his face.

Maybe change wasn't so bad after all.

"Soldier, Poet, King" by Savannah Coppersmith
Charlevoix High School, 12th Grade

We sat around my little wooden table, speaker blasting the songs from the "Oh Hellos" as we gathered 'round playing cards.

"So, what are you?" My friend asks.

"Well, I always thought I would be a poet or maybe the king."

"Nooo," she exclaims. "The quiz. Which one are you?"

I look at her quizzically, confused as to what she is alluding to. The song, "Soldier, Poet, King," just came up. I'd never thought too much about it- I know it has become popular but to me it's just a great song from one of my favorite bands. It dawns on me what she's talking about as she slips her phone into my hands. "Start Quiz" staring at me as I gaze at the screen.

At first I think it's a lighthearted quiz, then she informs me that your result is how your trauma manifests itself. That makes me a little nervous as I begin.

I recall this kid I knew from middle school. He was always falling asleep in class, and everyone assumed he just didn't care about school. I sat by him so I tried to befriend him whenever he seemed attentive. One day while we rode the bus home I casually asked why he was always so tired, thinking he would answer with something trivial like he was up playing video games.

But his eyes softened as he looked at me and he admitted that some nights he would come home and his father, "drunk as a skunk," he told me, would come after him with a belt for some made-up slight that he blamed his son for. So, my friend would sleep on the lawn, waiting till he heard the bus coming the next morning and groggily hustle aboard. That's why most nights he would get home as late as possible, when he could sneak in unseen.

I'm not typically one for physical affection but when he began to cry I hugged him. That day instilled more empathy into me, and I understood why he would jolt awake when someone would drop something in class, or why he would flinch when someone moved too quickly.

I moved away from that town but we still talk. He lives with his mother now and he has some anger issues, and he thinks everyone is out to get him, but he's learned to form outlets for his emotions. He designs fantastic 3D art, and when he's really worked up he'll go to the gym till he's too sore to willingly get out of bed the next day.

I sent him the quiz later that night. He got soldier.

My friend, the one watching me scroll through these questions, tells me proudly that she's a poet. Her eyes light up as she says it, and of course it's true. She's an artist, with stacks on stacks of lined paper, colorful sticky notes and Tul pens. She has beautiful writing that she's always giving me to proofread. Sometimes it's heartwarming, but it's also the expression of a hopeless romantic, rain splattering against the window and waiting for that special one.

Yet she's the sweetest person you'll ever meet. She loves to adopt little plants she'll add to her nook and she jams out to Taylor Swift on her record player, in her earbuds, anywhere she goes. I'll never have the stomach to tell her how insane her music drives me.

Sometimes people will yell around us and she gets real quiet. She stops fidgeting and goes still, sinking into some recess of her mind where I can't comfort her cause she stops hearing me. She'll crack jokes about how often she cries and how her therapist will be happy for her.

I think she first picked up a pen because she was too scared to grab the knife. I wonder if she's never put down that pen for fear of what might happen when she does. How many people are there who resorted to art because they knew they couldn't pull the trigger.

I answer the last question, hesitating a second before I click next. All the results seem appealing, but what I really want is the king, even though it probably fits what my friend's joke is my god complex. My finger taps the screen, the next page loads for a second before words flash before my eyes, "The King."

I turn the screen towards my friend. She gives a wise smile like she could've guessed so.

"Psychological," she tells me.

"What?"

"Psychological, that's the kind of trauma you have,"

I don't usually trust these quizzes as being at all accurate, but it looks like there has to be some truth to them. The king, head raised high, temper resolute, qualms hidden. I can see it.

One late night I sat in the backseat, watching the street pass me by. I no longer can recall why, but my father started arguing with my stepmom. They don't argue in front of me, so I was a little caught off guard. But I kept quiet as the tears fell down my face, my father's harsh voice struck something in me.

The scene brought me back to being with my then-step-father. He was a harsh alcoholic, and I used to stay awake at night listening to him yelling at my mother.

I'm learning to take things back for myself. I like to call myself a cynical romantic, for I often feel I possess a total lack of feeling thereof, yet there is a calmness and music that settles my soul.

In spite of my past, now I have a plan; I'm gonna carve out a piece of this world for myself to belong to, because if not me then who? My shoulders are burdened with many duties, but they keep me going and give me purpose. I'm no "king" but my ancestors were soldiers, poets, and kings. My story may not yet be told, but it has already begun to unfold.

Contributors

Storm Ainsely has lived in nine of the United States and will tell you she's from fiction-land. Her work has appeared in *Wild Roof Journal, Oakwood, Trace Fossils Review, Exist Otherwise*, and *West Trade Review* among others.

Kate Allore: Photographer, Poet, Potter Daughter, Wife, Mother, Grandmother — Devotee of heart opening beauty.

Margaret Anderson grew up in a large family whose father quoted poetry on a whim. She is a 2022 graduate of The Writer's Studio at Simon Fraser University. A Michigan native, Peggy resides in Vancouver, BC and is grateful to her supportive husband as she continues her writing journey.

Julie Angeli was born and raised in Michigan. Her work has appeared in children's literary magazines including *Spider* and *Cricket*, as well as adult anthologies including *Chicken Soup for the Soul* and *Sterling Script*. She loves paddleboarding and exploring Michigan's stunning shoreline.

Pamela Atsoff Native Michigander. Lifelong photo enthusiast. Lover of art and nature.

Michele Austin was raised in northern Wisconsin by native Yoopers. Michigan's Upper Peninsula is synonymous with "Happy" for her because of her large family there. Michele is a travel photographer, a published poet and essayist. Her first photography travelogue book is ready for publication.

Raegan Badik is fourteen years old, and in the 8th grade. She lives on Mackinac Island year-round with her family. Raegan enjoys reading, writing, art, dance, music, and theater.

Tom Barrat is a photographer specializing in travel, wildlife and architecture. With a portfolio of digital images from all over the United States and 40 countries, he is a contributing stock photographer to multiple stock agencies, as well as his own website, and publisher of high-quality coffee table books, such as *Up North Michigan.*

Elizabeth J. Bates is an amateur photographer who lives in Marquette, MI and enjoys capturing the 'visually interesting'. Her photos have graced the covers of Richard Rastall's anthology, *Maiden Voyage*, Milton Bates's collection of poems *Stand Still in the Light* and Edition 6 of *Walloon Writers Review*, as well as placing in local photo contests and exhibits.

Milton J. Bates is the author of the poetry collection *Stand Still in the Light* (2019) and two chapbooks, *Always on Fire* (2016) and *As They Were* (2018). His second collection, *Undivided Attention,* will appear in 2025.

Curt A. Benson is a Kent County Circuit Court judge and lifelong Michigan resident. He spends much of his spare time hiking, camping, fishing and hunting in northern Michigan.

Susan Boback lives in Michigan's Upper Peninsula, where she was born and raised. Inspired by community and conversation, she designs greeting cards, which she posts online, and writes oral history memoirs.

Jim Bolone is a native Michigander and has been a bartender, a drummer, a dockporter, a bouncer — most of these as a summer worker on Mackinac Island. For the past twenty-nine years, Jim has been a junior high English teacher in Northwest Ohio.

Monique Bova lives with her family in a cottage on the edge of the Pigeon River State Forest. When she's not at her desk job, she spends her time backpacking, contra dancing, learning to fly fish, tending a backyard garden, and raising two teenagers. The forests, rivers, and swamp bottoms of The Pigeon are where she finds most of her rejuvenation and inspiration.

Carrie Cantalupo writes poetry and flash fiction and has been published in *Pike's Peak, Making Waves, You Might Need to Hear This, Poetry Project Matters* and *Transformational: Stories of Northern Arts and Culture.* She is currently working on a hybrid chapbook. Carrie lives in Maple City in the Bohemian Wood and loves to hike, travel and read.

Nancy Carey lives on the South Arm of Lake Charlevoix in East Jordan. Her art is inspired by the daily changing faces of the waters and woods surrounding her home.

Tamar Charney is an Ann Arbor based journalist, writer, and photographer. Her writing and/or photography has been published by *Midwestern Gothic , Michigan Quarterly Review, Journal of Arts & Letters, Walloon Writers Review, NPR, Michigan Radio,* and *Public Radio International.*

Tom Conlan lives on a small farm in the highlands of Northern Michigan. His prose and poetry has appeared in numerous literary journals, including *Walloon Writers Review, QU Literary Review, UP Reader, Northwind Treasury, and Michigan Trout Magazine.* He is currently working on a poetry collection, *Secret Conversations.* Find his lyrical memoir *My Journey Begins Where the Road Ends...* and his novel, *Gentle Spirits* at thomasfordconlan.com.

Brenna Dean is a first-year Creative Writing master's student at Central Michigan University. She loves sitting in the sun with her kitten, watching movies with friends, visiting her dogs, and doing all sorts of crafts. She's always looking for another concert to attend with her best friends, another opportunity to write poems on Beaver Island, and another chance to look up at the moon and stars.

April DeOliveira is a Michigan-based writer and educator whose work has appeared in *Beyond Words Literary Magazine*, *Eunoia Review*, *Front Porch Republic*, *Great Lakes Review* (April Kragt), *Defenestrationism.net*, and others. When she is not feverishly pecking away on her tablet, she can be found reading, gardening, traversing the lovely state of Michigan with her wonderful husband, and wishing she weren't allergic to cats. Find more of her work at miraculousmundane.com.

Sarah DiViasmeṇi is a poet living on the shores of Lake Michigan. Some of her work can be found at thepoetess.substack.com.

Patty Durell (she/her) is a writer, sexual health educator, and fermentation enthusiast. She lives in Cheboygan, MI and spends as much time swimming as possible. Instagram.com/patty.pdf.

Elizabeth Fergus-Jean is a nationally recognized and award-winning transdisciplinary artist, educator and occasional writer whose focus is on the transformative and healing power of the creative spirit. She has been Artist-in-Residence at the Cincinnati Contemporary Arts Center, and at The Ohio State University; Elizabeth has taught for over 45 years including at the Columbus College of Art and Design, Denison University and Pacifica Graduate Institute, She holds an MFA in

Painting and Design from the University of Washington, and PhD in the Mythological Studies at Pacifica.

Katherine Foote is a senior at Central Michigan University studying English and Psychology. She is an aspiring writer who hopes to go on for her Master's and PhD in English Lit and to teach at the college level.

Lisa Fosmo is the author of a full-length collection of poetry *Mercy Is A Bright Darkness* published by Golden Dragonfly Press. Fosmo is a Pushcart prize nominated author, and the current vice president of the U.P. Poet Laureate Foundation.

Chris Gerst is a native of rural Michigan whose government career has taken him throughout the world making him fully able to attest; there's indeed, no place like home. When not in Michigan, he brings the north woods to his location with poetry and writing. Chris's latest work is *November Grey* (2024), a chapbook of poetry focused on the moods of this grey month and harbinger of winter.

CJ Giroux is a lifelong resident of Michigan. He teaches at Saginaw Valley State University and is a reader for *Dunes Review*.

Sheri Greene is a poet and a visual artist who resides in Grand Haven, Michigan. Sheri's poems have been published in *Walloon Writers Review, Peninsula Poets, TEN, Warren County Artists Market Anthology*. Beyond her creative pursuits, Sheri cherishes spending time with her family and enjoys showing and training her dogs, Lana and Lift and her horse, Swivel.

J. L. Hagen, writer, poet, and former non-profit executive, is the author of *Sea Stacks*, a short-story collection available on Amazon. His recent work, "Two Bells" (published in U. P. Reader #8), has been nominated for a Pushcart Prize. A graduate of University of Michigan and University of Chicago, he grew up in St. Ignace and currently lives in Southwest Michigan.

Nancy Hayes is an educator and artist living in northern Michigan. Her photographs capture light on landscape and water.

Betsy Hayhow Hemming enjoyed a varied career and now has returned to her roots as a writer. She crafts columns and essays about northern Michigan as well as short stories. She self-published her first novel, *William Bell* and now is working on a sequel. Visit her website at betsyhemming.com

Caroline Helmstadt is a writer and photographer from Saginaw, Michigan. She enjoys exploring the outdoors, especially that of northern Michigan, with her husband. To see more of her work, check out her page at Instagram.com/chelmstadt.

Deborah Hochberg is from Detroit, Michigan, and studied at Wayne State University. She has previously written about film for the *Detroit Metro Times* and is the author of two collections of poetry entitled *Waiting for the Snow* (Mission Point Press, 2021) and *Memory's Reservoir* (Mission Point Press, 2022).

Steve Hooper is a lifelong Yooper with too many hobbies. Some of his current creative endeavors include making outdoor adventure videos for his YouTube channel *Northern Waters*, writing about Michigan and the outdoors, and writing and performing music. saturdaysaunanight. wordpress.com.

Becky Jensen is a life-long Michigan resident, spoken word poet and proud mother of one. She enjoys exploring the wondrous beauty of the Great Lakes State, especially in the summer while looking for Petosky stones.

Now in his late seventies, **Hank Kaufmann** is a retired pipefitter and welder. During these contentious times he takes solace from family, friends, rescued animals, music (some of it self-inflicted), literature, and time in the outdoors.

Taylor Keiser shares: Backroads, shorelines, and sunlit trails are where I go to find solace, inspiration, and my innermost self. Northern Michigan's natural spaces have always embraced me (although not always warmly) when I needed them most."

Bridget Klaasen lives and writes in Suttons Bay, MI. She occasionally imagines herself somewhere else, but not for long. She considers it an honor to be included in this publication.

Mary Anna Scenga Kruch is a writer and photographer inspired by the natural world and her Italian ancestry past and present. She has published a poetry chapbook, a full-length hybrid memoir, and her latest collection, *Water Marks*. Maryannakruch.com.

Candace Lee has relished writing conferences with Jorie Graham, Susan Mitchell, Reginald Gibbons, William Shaw. She still enjoys homespun workshops with poets where metaphors spring forth as from a woodwind quintet. Her poetry has appeared in *Walloon Writers Review*, *The Prepress Awards Vol Two--Michigan Voices*, *the MacGuffin*, *Double Reed*, *Dunes Review* and elsewhere.

John Lennon is an English teacher and writer from Northern Michigan. Inspired by music and the beauty of everyday moments, his writing explores nature, human experience, and all the connections we have to the world around us. His work has appeared in *Walloon Writers Review*, the *Michigan English Teacher Newsletter*, and the *Language Arts Journal of Michigan*.

Kristin Bartley Lenz is a writer and social worker who divides her time between Metro Detroit and Walloon Lake. Her first novel, *The Art of Holding On and Letting Go*, was a Junior Library Guild Selection and a Great Lakes Great Books Award honor book. Find more of her writing at KristinBartleyLenz.com.

Jeanne Blum Lesinski writes when the mood strikes: sometimes that's 3 a.m., sometimes when singing while washing the dishes, sometimes on a bench at a Michigan beach. She only promises to not write while driving. She has prose and poetry in journals, anthologies, and online, and her debut poetry collection *Tethers End* appeared in 2023. Find out more about her work at jeanneblumlesinkiwriter.com.

Cassie Lindholm is a poet and bibliophile, a homebody and outdoor adventurer, a lover of slow mornings and night skies, a childless dog lady, a Michigander, and a forever tourist.

Ellen Lord is a Northern Michigan Native. Her writing has appeared in *Bear River Writers Review*, *Contemporary Haibun Online*, *Dunes Review*, *Walloon Writers Review*, *U.P. Reader*, *Frogpond*, *Failed Haiku* and elsewhere. She is a behavioral health therapist, specializing in addiction and trauma and resides in Charlevoix County and Trout Creek, Michigan. Her chapbook, *Relative Sanity* (2023) is available at ellenlordauthor.com.

Max Old Bear is a retired National Park Ranger with more than 40 years of service at Isle Royale, Everglades, Mount Rainier and Sleeping Bear Dunes. He has written a weekly nature column for the Leelanau Enterprise.

Amy Pendell helps people to reconnect with nature and themselves through her unique photography and art. A lover of our majestic universe, night and day, she lives in Michigan and treasures the natural beauty of this wonderful state. Instagram.com/amypendellart.

George Perreault has published five full-length collections of poetry and is the recipient of the inaugural Charles Simic Poetry Prize (2023). He is a direct descendant of Nicolas Perrot, a 17th century explorer of the Great Lakes region; there is a monument to Nicolas in Sault Ste. Marie, Ontario across from the Upper Peninsula.

Doug Pfaff is a writer, photographer and frustrated fly fisherman. He currently helps host the award-winning "Stacking Benjamins" podcast and lives with his wife and two dogs on a small lake south of Charlevoix. He's been exploring northern Michigan most of his life.

Anne M. Rashid grew up in Detroit, and, throughout her life, has enjoyed long visits to a family cabin in northern Michigan. She is Professor of English and Director of English and Women's and Gender Studies at Carlow University in Pittsburgh. She has published poetry in *Adagio Verse Quarterly, Lit Candles: Feminist Mentoring and the Text, The Metro Times, Pittsburgh's City Paper, Broad River Review, Paterson Literary Review, Pittsburgh Quarterly, The Fourth River and Sampsonia Way*, with work forthcoming in *The Gulf Tower Forecasts Rain*.

Karen Reasoner is the Creative Director at a graphic design company in Farmington Hills. Karen dabbles in fine art mediums from photography to water brush pens, colored pencils, to her favorite medium of oil pastels. She finds most of her fine art inspiration from nature, while hiking, running, and camping with her husband and dogs.

F.W. "Skip" Renker's poems have recently appeared in *Presence, Medvec, The Awakenings Review*, and several anthologies. His books are *Sifting the Visible* (Mayapple Press), *Bearing the Cast* (Saint Julian

Press), and *A Patient Hunger* (Atmosphere Press). Skip's MFA is from Seattle Pacific University, and he lives with his wife in the beautiful lakefront town of Petoskey, Michigan.

Jennifer Uehlein Reynolds of Charlevoix is an avid hiker and paddler who takes her camera wherever she goes. Her photos convey the landscapes and wildlife she encounters as they appear to her–no heavy editing or combining of images. Her goal is to encourage others to experience nature, and to provide experiences for those who might be unable to journey into the woods or onto the water. Follow her on Instagram at jenren_hikes.

Katherine Roth lives and works as a collaborating physician in Traverse City, Michigan. Her poetry has been published in *Wild Root Journal, Walloon Writers Review, Open Palm Print, Contemporary Halibun* and the *Peninsula Poets*. She is the co-author of the memoir *The Good Fight: A Story of Love, Cancer and Triumph*. Her poetry collection is entitled *Unforgotten*.

David James "DJ" Savarese is the author of *Swoon* and *A Doorknob for the Eye*, co-author of *Studies in Brotherly Love*, and the co-producer, narrator, poet of the Peabody award-winning documentary *Deej: Inclusion Shouldn't Be a Lottery*. His poems and lyric essays have appeared in *A Hole in the Wall, Bellingham Review, Iowa Review, Nine Mile Magazine, Poem-A Day, Poetry Foundation, Poets.org, Red Wheelbarrow, Seneca Review, Split This Rock, Stone Canoe, The Art of Autism, Walloon Writers Review* and *Wordgathering*. www.djsavarese.com

Ralph James Savarese is a Professor of English at Grinnell College. He is the author of *Reasonable People: A Memoir of Autism and Adoption* (Other Press 2007); *Republican Fathers* (Nine Mile Books 2020); *When This Is Over: Pandemic Poems* (Ice Cube Press 2020); Co-editor,

"Autism and the Concept of Neurodiversity," a special issue of Disability Studies Quarterly (2010) as well as numerous publications regarding neurodiversity and autism.

Gary Schils taught theatre, dance and music to children of all ages for twenty four years and more. His mission was to inspire creativity and imagination. Currently his new passion is carving wood, mostly indigenous fish and shore birds.

Scot Siegel is a city planner, educator, and author of four full-length books of poetry, most recently, *Tender Currencies* (MoonPath Press, 2025), and *The Constellation of Extinct Stars and Other Poems*, (Salmon Poetry, 2016). Siegel is the recipient of the 2024 Sally Albiso Poetry Book Award, and has received fellowship residencies through Oregon State University, and Playa at Summer Lake, among others. Scot's family is from Michigan, and for many years his grandpa operated a hunting lodge on the Au Sable River. scotsiegel.com.

Northwest Michigan has been **Michael Sipkoski's** home for a decade. His interests run through literature, photography, classical guitar, conservation, fooling wild trout, hiking and otherwise finding beauty and surprise in Michigan's waters, woods, and terrain. He has contributed to *The Boardman Review*, *Michigan Trout*, and *Walloon Writers Review*.

Kirk Small lives with his soul mate and their ill-mannered dog in Bellaire Michigan. Kirk loves and hates rehabbing his 90 year old field stone cottage, worries over each sentence he writes, and hopes to successfully pen stories that reflect the joy, love and sorrow that we all share. The short story, "Water Speaks", is adapted from the soon to be completed novel entitled *Water Speaks and Leaves Fall*.

Don Spezia has been interested in photography, since acquiring his first 35mm camera. Photographs usually include nature, wildlife, architecture, moments,, motion, and landscapes. His favorite photographs are outdoors, influenced by the elements of nature. His photography has been accepted at various juried art & photography exhibits. He worked as an Architect as his career and retired in 2017. More information about Don's photography & guitar music can be found at donspezia-friznicmusic.com.

K. Matthew Springfield was born and raised in Michigan, and currently resides in Clawson. He views every trip he takes afield as an opportunity to learn something new and believes that the outdoors are for everyone. He can be found most weekends exploring his home state's lesser-known public lands and waters.

Ellen Schettling Whitehead "We all face challenges in life. I have found that being still and noticing simple, everyday beauty around me helps me overcome challenges and brings me peace. I especially find this peace in nature, writing poetry, and taking photos."